A FORGE OF
FREEDOM BOOK

The Thirteen Colonies
~1763~

The New Jersey Colony

FRED J. COOK

CROWELL-COLLIER PRESS

Collier-Macmillan Limited, London

PICTURE CREDITS

Culver Pictures, Inc., 3, 14, 17, 34–35, 62, 85, 90, 101, 111, 116, 124; Historical
Pictures Service—Chicago, 13, 87, 92–93; New Jersey Department of Conserva-
tion and Economic Development, 118; New Jersey Historical Society, 22–23, 38,
45, 46, 70–71, 72, 73, 74, 79, 81, 120, 122–123, 126; New Jersey State Museum
(*New Jersey's Indians* by Dorothy Cross), 6; Salem County Historical Society, 40.

JACKET ILLUSTRATION: The arrest of Governor Philip Carteret

CONTENTS

one

The
Accidental Colony

New Jersey was an accident among the Thirteen Colonies. In most cases, settlers set out from Europe with a definite purpose. They came to seek religious freedom, to find gold or to make fortunes from fur trading. New Jersey, however, did not attract direct settlement. It was occupied and developed piecemeal—a fur-trading post here, a lonely cluster of cabins there—by wanderers who spilled over into it from nearby colonies.

As a result of this accidental birth, the colony was from the first a mixture of many peoples and many faiths. There were Swedes in South Jersey, Dutch in North Jersey; and scattered throughout both sections were all kinds of English—peace-loving Quakers, fiery Puritans and rebels against Puritan ideas.

Such a mixture created many problems, and so for years New Jersey was really two colonies instead of one. The southern part below a diagonal line that ran from Egg

Harbor on the coast to the vicinity of the Delaware Water Gap was called West Jersey; the northern part, East Jersey. Even after the two parts had been joined into one whole, documents for years referred to "the Jerseys" as if they were two separate provinces.

The first written record we have of any great exploration of New Jersey dates back to the voyage of Henry Hudson in the *Half Moon* in 1609. Hudson was the British sailor and navigator who had been hired by the Dutch East India Company to try to find what all men from the time of Columbus had sought—a westward passage to the riches of China and the Orient. During the summer of 1609, Hudson cruised along the Atlantic coast as far south as Cape Hatteras, seeking a break in the wall of the continent. Failing to find the channel he sought, he turned north and crept in closer to the shore, studying the bays and inlets. At the end of August, he poked the *Half Moon*'s nose into Delaware Bay, at the same time spying land to the north which he took to be an island, but which was really Cape May.

Hudson named the Delaware the South River, but he found that it had many treacherous shoals, and so he did not go up it for any great distance. Instead, he put out to sea and turned north again. Robert Juet, his first mate, who kept a journal of the voyage, wrote: "The Sunne arose, and we steered away North againe, and saw the Land from the West by North, to North-west by North, all like broken Ilands. . . ."

The "broken Ilands" that Juet mentioned were the chain of sandy, offshore islands sheltering a whole network of bays and rivers along the southern New Jersey coast. To Hudson this was "a drowned land with trees behind it."

On September 2, 1609, Hudson and his men sighted the low, gleaming spit of Sandy Hook. High behind rose the Navesink hills of northern Monmouth County. Rounding the hook, Hudson entered the waters of New York harbor

Indians paddled out from the New Jersey shore to see the Half Moon

and began the exploration of the mouth of the great river to which he was to give his name. Robert Juet, impressed by the magnificent harbor and the forest-clad Jersey hills, wrote in his journal: "This is a very good land to fall in with, and a pleasant land to see."

Indians paddled out from the Jersey shore in their birch-bark canoes, and some of them boarded the *Half Moon.* Juet noted, with a touch of the white man's greed, that many wore ornaments that gleamed like "yellow copper."

On September 5, part of the crew landed and spent the day rambling across the untouched Monmouth hills. They were impressed by the size of oaks "of a height and thickness that are seldom beheld," and they admired the graceful linden trees, the huge blue plums, and the red and white vines that flourished in the ancient forests. They gathered some "whortleberries," or huckleberries, and Juet pronounced them "sweet and good."

Hudson went on up the river as far as Albany before finally sailing for home. In Holland, his account of his discoveries sparked immediate interest. Fortunes were to be made in those days in fur trading, and Hudson's account of a primitive forest teeming with beaver and other fur-bearing animals roused the trader's appetite in the Dutch. The very next year, 1610, an expedition was sent from Holland to make use of Hudson's discoveries. Soon Dutch fur-trading posts, extending up the Hudon River to Albany, were sending back thousands of valuable pelts to Holland.

New Jersey, in the meantime, lay largely neglected. It was still the preserve of the Indians—and there were, in the entire state, only about one thousand of them. These were divided roughly into three bands, all members of the Lenni-Lenapé, or Delaware, tribe.

The first of these Indian clans lived in the upper Delaware Valley, among the high hills of what are now Warren, Morris and Sussex Counties. They were known as the Minsi, or Mountaineers, and their totem, or symbol, was the wolf. They were the fiercest fighters, the real warriors, of the Lenni-Lenapé.

Farther down the Delaware, scattered along its banks, lived the second of the three Indian divisions, known as the Unami or People down the River. Their totem was the tortoise, and they were said to be the wisest of the New Jersey Indians in council.

The third and last of the Indian clans was the Unalachtigo, or the People Who Live near the Ocean. These Indians were scattered along the coast down to Cape May. They were noted for their skill in fishing, and they were also much gentler than the more warlike Minsi of the northern mountains. For this reason, they were looked down upon with contempt by the fierce Iroquois tribes of New York state, who regarded all Lenni-Lenapé as "old women."

These New Jersey Indians were of medium height, dark-eyed and dark-haired. They lived a primitive life. They had no permanent villages and no large, central community houses as did the Indians of New York. Their homes were wigwams, which soon became incredibly dirty from the garbage of cooking and the litter of animals. When the smell and filth became too much, the Indian simply moved his wigwam to a new place. The New Jersey Lenni-Lenapé were largely nomads. They were constantly changing their hunting and fishing sites with the seasons. Spring and summer would find most of the families moving to new camp-sites along the rivers, bays and ocean. Winter would find them seeking shelter, fuel and warmth in the deep woods.

Their clothing was made of hides, tanned and decorated with various designs. Their weapons and utensils were made from rock and bone. Large bones were used to scratch the earth to plant the few crops, mainly corn and beans, that they grew. Smaller bones were used for needles, fish hooks and ornaments. Pieces of rock were chipped to make crude knives, chisels, net sinkers, fish spears and arrow-heads. The bow and arrow was, of course, the weapon on which the Indians depended for hunting.

Clay was used to make bowls, jars and dishes. The clay would be worked into the desired shape and then sun-baked until it was hard enough for use. Strings of wampum were used for ornaments. The wampum was made from the white and black parts of clam and oyster shells, ground into round shapes, pierced and strung into bracelets that could be worn on the arms or legs. Some of the Indians boasted flashier ornaments—those pieces of copper, taken from the hills of Essex County or the Valley of the Raritan, that had caught the eye of Henry Hudson's mate, Robert Juet.

Though the life of these Lenni-Lenapé lacked all comforts, food was seldom a problem. The woods, the rivers, the very air were alive. Great schools of whales paraded along the coast and even poked their noses into the deep bays, spouting streams of vapor high into the air when they breathed. The waters that almost surrounded the state were alive with all kinds of fish, rich with almost endless quantities of clams, oysters, shrimp and lobsters. The woods were filled with deer, wolves, bear, wild turkeys. One early English explorer marveled at having shot a wild turkey that weighed forty-six pounds. There were, in addition, such swarms of swans, geese and ducks that they turned the air

These copper ornaments, unearthed recently in New Jersey, are like those that caught the eye of Robert Juet

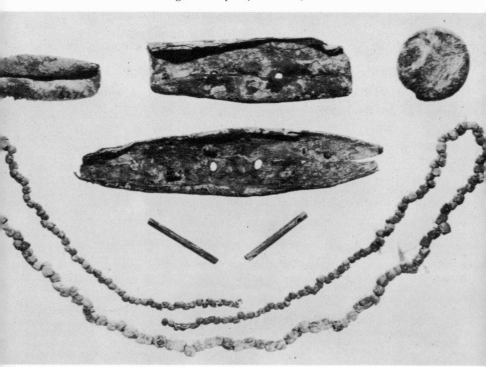

almost black during their yearly fall migrations to the south.

Such was the unspoiled land, bursting with natural riches, to which the first white men came, setting up small trading posts to deal with the Indians.

The first settlers in south Jersey were not English, not Dutch—but Swedes. The reports of Hudson and other explorers of a vast, rich and untamed land sparked great competition among European nations. Each was eager to seize a portion of this new world for itself. Sweden at the time was under the rule of one of her greatest kings, Gustavus Adolphus, and he decided to attempt to establish a colony in America.

Urging the King on in this endeavor was William Usselinx, a merchant of Antwerp who had originally been employed by the Dutch. Usselinx was joined by Peter Minuit, who had been the first governor of the Dutch colony of New Netherland (now New York), and who had also fallen out with his Dutch employers. Commercial companies were formed with the King's backing, and in December, 1637, the first Swedish expedition sailed for the New World.

It was sometime in March, 1638, that Peter Minuit in the man-of-war *Kalmar Nyckel,* followed by a smaller vessel, entered the Delaware, which the Swedes named New Swedeland Stream. A landing was made at Murderkill Creek in the southern part of what is now the state of Delaware. The Swedish colonists bargained with the Indians and bought from them a tract of land on the site of the present city of Wilmington. Here Peter Minuit built a fort that he called Fort Christina.

Minuit shortly afterward lost his life in a storm in the West Indies, but other expeditions continued to sail from Sweden for a number of years, bringing more colonists. Additional lands were purchased from the Indians, extending the boundaries of New Sweden along the Delaware to a point opposite the present city of Trenton. The Swedes also began to establish small footholds on the New Jersey side of the river, building Fort Nya Elfsborg on the river between Salem and Alloways Creek in 1643. By 1644 there were about two hundred Swedish colonists in the settlements along the Delaware, but only a handful had established themselves on the New Jersey shore.

Now, for the first time, the English began to show an interest in this great, almost unsettled tract of land that lay between the Delaware and the Atlantic Ocean.

In 1632 a group of noblemen headed by Sir Edmund Plowden, of Ireland, sought permission to establish a colony on Long Island. After much dickering at court, they were finally granted a patent by King Charles I. The grant was a noble one. Plowden was named the first governor of an immense tract of land that included, not only Long Island, but what are now the states of New Jersey, Delaware, Maryland and Pennsylvania. He called this new empire New Albion.

Plowden had planned to send out five hundred colonists, but there was much delay and arguing among the supporters of his plan. Finally, in 1634, a single ship was sent out not to set up a colony but to explore and try to find a route to the Indies. The expedition was commanded by Captain Thomas Yong who had with him as his first lieutenant his nephew, Robert Evelin. Yong and Evelin reached the Delaware in August, 1634. They named the river the Charles after the English king, and they explored it as far north as Trenton, where rocks and rapids barred their further progress. Evelin then went back down the river and explored the coast from Cape May to Sandy Hook.

Yong and Evelin were apparently so enchanted by the land that they spent the next seven years along the Delaware. They sent glowing reports back to England about the wonderful country that they had found. But their colorful descriptions failed to rouse any enthusiasm among the English lower classes to colonize New Albion for Earl Plowden. Unable to get the colonists he needed, Plowden finally set out in 1642 to see for himself the empire he had been granted.

His expedition was a disaster. The Swedes by this time were well established along the Delaware, and they naturally refused to accept Plowden's authority. They also refused to let English ships trade in the Delaware. Plowden's own people mutinied and marooned him and two young followers on an island in Delaware Bay. The Swedes kindly rescued them, recovered the vessel the mutineers had seized from Plowden and sent the Earl and his party packing back to England.

There, Plowden made another effort in 1650 to gather one hundred and fifty colonists for his promised land. But he found that he just could not interest the British people. They would brave the stormy Atlantic, the wilderness and the Indians in search of religious or political freedom, but they simply would not take such risks to help a nobleman carve out for himself a private state in the New World. Plowden kept trying until he died in 1659, but he was never able to make his "New Albion" a reality. With his death, his claim to a private empire in the New World lapsed. And the Swedes and Dutch were left to wrestle for the prize of that untamed land that was to become known as New Jersey.

two

The
Dutch

Northern New Jersey, today an area of smoking factories and smelly chemical works, was a green paradise when the Dutch first settled New Amsterdam, as they called what is now the city of New York.

Lured by Henry Hudson's account of a great river that ran into the heart of fur-trapping country, the Dutch lost no time in crossing the Atlantic and taking almost instant possession of the New York harbor area. By 1614 they had established themselves firmly on the island of Manhattan, now the business heart of New York. Each year they explored farther along the New Jersey coast.

In 1621 Captain Cornelis Jacobsen Mey entered the South River, as the Dutch called the Delaware, and gave his name to the long peninsula that juts out into Delaware Bay. Mey built a fort that he called Fort Nassau, near what is now Red Bank on the Jersey side of the Delaware—a tiny and temporary Dutch outpost in what was soon to become Swedish territory.

The Dutch were far too few in numbers to colonize land along both the North River (the name they gave the Hudson) and the Delaware. And so they used their efforts for several years to strengthen their grip on the New York–Hudson River area.

As early as 1618 the Dutch had built a fort on the present site of Albany, and in the early 1620s they replaced this with a stronger one that they called Fort Orange. All of this was done by traders and merchants acting on their own, without any central authority. But, in 1626, the Dutch West India Company decided that the development of its colony of New Netherland would have to be put on a more formal basis, and so Peter Minuit was sent as the first governor.

Minuit, following the Dutch custom, met with the Indians and, for about twenty-four dollars in trade goods, purchased from them the whole of Manhattan Island. Here he erected a fort and founded the village that he called New Amsterdam.

The Dutch tried again in 1632 to establish a colony at Cape May, but there was trouble with the Indians, and the attempt was abandoned. Much more successful was the thrust into those green pastures of northern New Jersey so close at hand.

The richness of this land beckoned the Dutch from their first days in New Amsterdam. Wide meadows full of high, waving grass stretched from the banks of the Passaic, the Elizabeth and the Raritan rivers. On hills behind, back from the river banks, towered huge trees in forests untouched for centuries.

"This is the handsomest and pleasantest country a man can behold," Secretary Van Tienhoven, of the New Netherland colony, wrote in 1650. "It furnished the Indians with abundance of maize, beans, pumpkins and other fruits."

Some twenty years later, one of the first English settlers was equally enthusiastic. Even if a man had hundreds of cattle, he wrote, "he need not fear their want of pasture in the summer or fodder in the winter. . . . You have grass as high as a man's knees . . . and these woods also every mile or half-mile are furnished with fresh ponds, brooks and rivers, where all sorts of cattle during the heat of the day do quench their thirst and cool themselves."

In this lovely region, the Dutch now made their settlements. Their first outpost on the New Jersey side of the Hudson was at Hoboken, called by the Indians Hobocan-hackingh—the place of the tobacco pipe. As the name indicates, this was the place where the Indians and Dutch traders met, smoked the peace pipe, and swapped furs for the gew-gaws the Indians wanted. Though Hoboken remained largely a trading post, other settlements at Bergen, Wee-hawken and parts of Jersey City, all established during the 1630s, turned to farming, brewing and other pursuits.

The settlers' relationship with the Indians was friendly at first, but in 1643 the greed and stupidity of a Dutch governor in New Amsterdam brought tragedy. In February of that year, the Tappan Indians, who occupied the land in the vicinity of the New Jersey settlements, were suddenly attacked by the more warlike Mohawk tribe to the north. Routed by the Mohawks, they fled for protection to their Dutch friends in the Communipaw settlement, now a part of Jersey City.

In New Amsterdam, Governor William Kieft apparently saw in these developments an opportunity to wipe out the Tappan Indians and seize their lands. And so, on the night of February 27, 1643, eighty Dutch soldiers under a Sergeant Rudolf quietly crossed the Hudson and fell upon the sleeping Indians. They slaughtered eighty, sparing not even the women and children, and dumped their bodies into one long burial pit.

The few Indians who were lucky enough to escape the slaughter thought at first that they had been attacked again by the Mohawks. Leaping into their birchbark canoes, they paddled across the Hudson to New Amsterdam. There they appealed to Kieft for protection. And the merciless governor ordered them slain to the last man.

There followed a savage Indian war. Tribes went on the warpath from the Raritan River to Connecticut. They burned cabins and farms, killed the male settlers, and dragged women and children off into captivity. They even stole into the streets of New Amsterdam, burning and looting. One account of the time says, "Not a white person was safe except, indeed, those who sought and found refuge within the palisades of Fort Amsterdam."

Eventually, the Indian attack spent its fury, peace was restored, and Dutch settlers crept cautiously back to the blackened farm sites on the New Jersey meadows from which they had been driven. It was, fortunately, the last time that they were to be seriously molested by the Indians.

Kieft's bungling and treachery, the cause of the disaster, led to his dismissal as governor. He was succeeded by a stern, one-legged warrior, Peter Stuyvesant. Stuyvesant arrived in New Amsterdam May 11, 1647, and promptly restored order.

The new governor's rule was often harsh. He was the kind of rough soldier who could not stand a rival, and the presence of the Swedes along the Delaware annoyed him. He was especially angered when the Swedes refused to let a Dutch sloop trade along the river. They also barred the Dutch from hunting for minerals in the vicinity of Trenton.

Though these actions seemed to say that the Swedes would stand for no competition along the Delaware, the

One-legged Peter Stuyvesant

Swedish colonists were being gradually cut off from their homeland. Sweden had suffered severe setbacks in the bloody European wars then raging. It was no longer able to keep sending yearly expeditions, with supplies of guns and ammunition, to the settlers in the New World. Yet, without such supplies, the Swedes could hardly hope to stand off the growing power of the Dutch.

In 1651, Stuyvesant decided that the time had come to strike. He sent a warship by sea to Cape May, and he marched overland through the New Jersey wilderness at the head of one hundred and twenty men. Uniting his sea and land forces, Stuyvesant swept the lower reaches of the Delaware and built Fort Casimir near what is now New Castle, Delaware.

Though there was peace for a time, the new fort and the Dutch presence on the lower river menaced Swedish trade.

And so the Swedes gambled in 1654, attacking Fort Casimir and capturing it. Stuyvesant, when he heard the news, was furious.

He assembled what, for that time and place, was a powerful armada—seven war vessels and some seven hundred soldiers. In 1655, he sailed into the Delaware, seeking battle with the Swedes. They, however, were in no shape to resist. Stuyvesant's force was overwhelming, and the Swedes surrendered. New Sweden died and became for nearly ten years part of the Dutch colony of New Netherland.

While the Swedes and Dutch were fighting with each other for footholds on the American continent, the English had not been idle. They had founded colonies in Virginia, in Massachusetts, in Rhode Island and Connecticut. Now the geography of the situation made them worry. The strong and growing Dutch colony that included New York, New Jersey and Delaware was like a dagger thrust into the very heart of their holdings. If the Dutch retained their possessions, they were a foreign wedge separating the English colonies in New England from the English colonies in the South. This was a situation that the English were determined to correct.

When relations with Holland worsened to the point of war, the English decided to strike. King Charles II paved the way by making his brother, James, Duke of York, the proprietor of a vast section of the American continent. James was given what is now Maine, Long Island, the islands Martha's Vineyard and Nantucket, and all that huge region lying between the Connecticut River and the Delaware. This included part of the state of Connecticut and all of New York and New Jersey.

The very nature of this sprawling, disconnected grant made little sense and was to be the cause of much confusion. But at the moment this did not matter. The Duke of York, having been given the properties of the Dutch by his brother, determined to make the gift good by seizing them. He assembled a fleet and sent it off to America to attack New Netherland.

The Duke's commander was Richard Nicolls, whom he named deputy governor to rule the province once it was taken. Nicolls, after gathering some reinforcements in Boston, arrived off New York on August 18, 1664. Peter Stuyvesant and the Dutch had little with which to oppose him. Fort Amsterdam was weak and in bad repair. There was little ammunition and few provisions to carry the colony through a siege. The powerful British warships promptly seized full control of the waterways by which Manhattan is surrounded.

Nicolls called on Stuyvesant to surrender. The grumpy old soldier wanted to fight, but the Dutch burghers in New Amsterdam would have none of it. And so finally, on September 3, 1664, Stuyvesant surrendered the town and colony to the British. New Amsterdam was promptly renamed New York in honor of the Duke of York, and the region between the Hudson and the Delaware was called Albania. It was a name that it was not to bear for long.

Though Nicolls did not know it at the time, his royal master had already made separate plans for this territory. Shortly after receiving his grant from the King, the Duke of York had given away what is now New Jersey. He made a present of the state to two loyal followers who had sided with the royal family during the English civil war in which King Charles I had been beheaded. The lucky pair so richly rewarded were Lord John Berkeley and Sir George Carteret.

Carteret especially had distinguished himself during the civil war. He had seized the Island of Jersey in the English Channel and had held it for the King, the last royal outpost in the British Isles. In memory of this feat, the Duke of York ordered that the proprietors' new holdings should be called New Caesaria or New Jersey. So the colony got its name.

Charles II gave his brother James, Duke of York, all of New Jersey

It got much else besides. From the beginning, there was trouble. The holdings of Berkeley and Carteret were soon divided, with Berkeley taking over the southern and western part of the state; Carteret, the northern and eastern section. This was the beginning of the division of New Jersey into what for a long time were two separate provinces—East and West Jersey.

There were other complications. In New York, Governor Nicolls was acting in the belief that he ruled New Jersey. He was granting settlers titles to land—but the land, unknown to him, had already been given to Berkeley and Carteret by the Duke of York, and only they could legally transfer title to it. So was laid the basis of conflict. It was a conflict that was to keep New Jersey in turmoil for the next century; a conflict that laid the seeds of revolt and paved the way for the Revolution.

three  Religious
Persecution

Even before the English took New Netherland from the
Dutch in 1664, settlers had been coming into New Jersey
from the English colonies in New England. They were
driven by the same force that had led to the settlement of
the nothern colonies—religious persecution.

The Puritans who landed at Plymouth Rock and later
set up the Massachusetts Bay Colony were fleeing from
harsh treatment in their homeland, but they were themselves strict, harsh and sometimes cruel. The "freedom"
that they sought was freedom for themselves alone. They
insisted that all who came and settled in Massachusetts must
believe as the Puritans believed and worship as the Puritans
worshiped. All others were heretics to be beaten and sometimes hanged.

Two religious faiths especially aroused the hatred of the
Puritans. There were the Baptists, who believed that men
had a right to worship God in their own individual ways,

and there were the Quakers, those disturbing people who took literally the Biblical command to turn the other cheek —and so refused to bear arms, to fight, or to take an oath of allegiance to any ruler.

Efforts of the Baptists and the Quakers to worship in their own ways—and to encourage others to do so—led to the passage of severe laws. Punishments such as whipping, banishment and execution were provided. Enforcement was strict, even savage. When one offender lay dying from 117 blows upon his back with a tarred rope, the Reverend John Norton denounced him to pitying bystanders in these words: "He endeavored to beat the gospel ordinance black and blue, and it was but just to beat him black and blue."

The persecution of the Baptists and Quakers became so severe that in 1660 King Charles II banned all executions for religious purposes in his dominions. But the Baptists and Quakers were still subjected to heavy fines, flogging and other punishments. Seeking a freer land, many fled to Long Island, where the Dutch were noted for their tolerance of various religious faiths. But this open-mindedness did not apply to Quakers.

Peter Stuyvesant was hardly the man to welcome a cult that would not bear arms or fight or take an oath of allegiance. Again the Quakers suffered imprisonment, fines, whippings.

Suffering from much brutality, the Baptists and Quakers turned their eyes to the west, to the green meadows of New Jersey. In 1663 a scouting party of some twenty persons of the two faiths sailed from Long Island to the northern Monmouth County shore. There, despite the protest of Dutch traders, they made a deal with the Indians for a large tract of land along the Navesink and Shrewsbury rivers. Early the following year, John Bowne, Richard Stout and others founded the villages of Middletown and Shrewsbury. The Baptists settled around Middletown; the Quakers, at Shrewsbury. Many of the new settlers in both towns were those who had been imprisoned or had felt the savage lash of the whip in New England.

The homes of these first settlers were crude, not much better than the Indians' wigwams. Sometimes a tent-shaped "house" would be made by bending the tops of young saplings and tying them together. Then the sides of the crude structure so created would be filled in with sod and straw, making rough walls to keep out the biting winter winds. Other "homes" were made by digging cellar-like holes in the ground. The floors and walls of such holes would be covered with rough-hewn planks. For roofs, A-frames made of poles would be pitched together, covered with bark and sod.

Life was cruel and hard, but the new settlers felt that they were finally free. The Dutch, though they were not too happy about it, had approved the purchase of land from the Indians by the Baptists and Quakers. It seemed that the settlers could look forward to building their own communities in their own way. But then, suddenly, everything was changed. The Dutch were conquered, and the English ruled. What would this new rule be like?

Berkeley and Carteret, the new proprietors of "the Jerseys," had no intention of abandoning the pleasures of the King's court for a hard life in the wilderness. They sent out as their first governor Sir George Carteret's cousin, Captain Philip Carteret, a young man only twenty-six years of age.

In April, 1665, young Carteret sailed on the ship *Philip* with about thirty persons, gentlemen and their servants, most of them from the Channel Islands. Carteret landed first in Virginia and stayed there for several weeks. He sent Governor Nicolls in New York word of his arrival—the first notice Nicolls had that New Jersey had been given away and that he no longer ruled it. This confused situation was to have far-reaching effects, for Nicolls had been trying to encourage settlement in New Jersey. He had, indeed, just approved the sale of Indian lands to four Long Island families. Soon after, when Philip Carteret reached New York harbor on July 29, 1665, he found these families setting up homesteads. Philip named the place Elizabethtown after Lady Elizabeth Carteret, Sir George's wife. The land grant made by Nicolls became known as the Elizabethtown Purchase.

This, then, was the situation as Philip Carteret found it:

There were four families just setting up home sites at Elizabethtown. There were Dutch families, perhaps two hundred persons in all, living in the tiny villages of Hoboken, Bergen and Weehawken. There were the Baptist and Quaker settlements at Middletown and Shrewsbury. And beyond these was a howling wilderness until one reached the Delaware. There again one found small handfuls of Dutch at Burlington and a few Swedes and Dutch along the lower Delaware.

Two issues concerned these settlers most. What about the titles to their lands—would these be good under the new proprietors? And what kind of government would the proprietors establish—would it grant them the freedom and privileges they had sought?

The answer to the second question seemed much clearer than the answer to the first. After the Duke of York had made Berkeley and Carteret a present of New Jersey, the new proprietors had drawn up a document they called Concessions and Agreements. They seemed to have thought that it would be impossible (as Earl Plowden had found out in his futile attempt to settle South Jersey) to get colonists to risk all the dangers and hardships of the wilderness if they were to remain mere servants under English gentle-

men-masters. If the new proprietors were to get colonists to settle their lands, they would have to offer the reward of broad freedoms. And so the Concessions and Agreements they drew up were generous.

First of all, they guaranteed full religious freedom. They also provided for liberal land grants. Every freeman sailing with the first governor was promised one hundred and fifty acres, provided he equipped himself with "a good musket" and the necessary powder and ball. He could claim additional acres for each servant he brought with him. The government was to be quite democratic. The proprietors would appoint the governor, and the governor in turn would name a council of advisers to help him. The governor and his council alone would have the power to appoint law-enforce-

Philip Carteret, appointed governor of the Colony of New Jersey, landed at Newark Bay in 1665

ment officers. Offsetting these powers was the provision for an assembly. The settlers themselves were to choose the assembly, and this body held important powers. It alone could make laws, set up courts—and, most important, levy taxes for defense and the support of the government. This grip on the purse strings meant that the governor himself could not be paid unless the assembly voted him the money for his salary. New Jersey assemblies, for the next century, were to use this money power to insure popular rule.

Two other provisions in the Concessions and Agreements did not sit so well with the new settlers. One provided that inhabitants of the colony, to have the other rights offered them, must take an oath of allegiance to the King and pledge faithfulness to the proprietors. This provision bothered the Quakers, who opposed oaths of allegiance to any worldly power. The second unpopular requirement called for the payment of a quit rent to the proprietors. The quit rent was a hangover from the Middle Ages. It represented originally the payment a tenant made to his lord in return for the lord's protection against possible attackers. In New Jersey, the quit rent to be paid the proprietors was only a halfpenny an acre, beginning in 1670. But, as the settlers were quick to point out, the proprietors guaranteed them no protection. The settlers had to provide their own. The payment of a quit rent was unfair.

Land titles provided an equally disturbing issue. It was one that faced Philip Carteret the day he set foot on New Jersey soil and found four families settling Elizabethtown by right of their land grant from Nicolls and purchase from the Indians. Also as part of the surrender agreement with the Dutch, Nicolls had agreed to recognize the land titles of the Middletown and Shrewsbury settlers. And he had held some discussions with a new group of colonists who wanted to come to New Jersey.

These pilgrims were from New Haven, Connecticut. New Haven had been founded by Puritans of the most extreme type. So fanatical were they, indeed, that only church members could vote, make laws and perform public duties. They proclaimed that "the word of God shall be the only rule attended unto in ordering the affairs of government." In other words, New Haven was a Bible state, its government in the hands of a small church group working closely with the clergy.

Before long, however, the younger generation in New Haven rebelled against this strict church rule. Uniting with more liberal people in the town, they forced through the town meeting a series of laws that stripped the church elders of much of their governmental powers. The older Puritans were unwilling to accept this state of affairs. They began looking for a new country where they could practice the "pure" religion. Their search led them to New Jersey.

It is one of the most striking oddities in the history of the state that the Baptists and Quakers who settled Middletown and Shrewsbury were driven into New Jersey by the harshness of Puritan doctrine. The settlers from New Haven came for the opposite reason: because they felt their old, strict faith had been undermined by new, youth-inspired ideas.

The New Haven group at first considered settling along the Delaware. After discussions with Philip Carteret, however, they agreed to make their new homes along the Passaic River in northern New Jersey. In May, 1666, they left New Haven and established a settlement on the site of what was to become Newark, New Jersey's largest city today. In December, 1666, other groups from Massachusetts settled Piscataway and Woodbridge.

The land in all of these settlements had been included in that vast tract known as the Elizabethtown Purchase. This was the grant that Governor Nicolls of New York had approved before Philip Carteret arrived on the scene. The new settlers, indeed, acquired the acres needed for their towns by buying them from the Elizabethtown Associates, and Governor Carteret did not dispute this arrangement. He even bought for his own use one tract of land from the Elizabethtown Associates, and he had a hand in arranging for the sales to the Newark, Piscataway and Woodbridge settlers.

The new pioneers, therefore, had every right to feel that they owned their homes and that the titles to them did not depend on Lord Berkeley and Sir George Carteret, those distant proprietors in England. Berkeley and Carteret, on the other hand, felt that they owned all of New Jersey because the Duke of York had given it to them. They believed that all who had not bought land from them were illegal squatters on their property.

Here was the making of a heated argument. The issue of land titles—and with it, the claim that all must pay quit rents to Berkeley and Carteret, the distant proprietors— soon sparked fierce and violent rebellion among the independent New Jersey settlers.

four

The First Rebellions

The early settlers of New Jersey, whatever their religious faiths, were a sturdy and independent group. Their independence was what had brought them to this colony in the first place. It was this that had made them risk much, suffer much, on what was an outermost frontier of their time. These risks and sufferings, added to their natural independence, made them a quarrelsome sort, ready to fight at the first threat to any of their cherished liberties.

The entirely unplanned manner in which New Jersey had been settled made conflict certain. Take, for example, the Monmouth patent, granted by Governor Nicolls before the arrival of Philip Carteret. This authorized the Middletown and Shrewsbury settlers not just to hold town meetings, but to have a general assembly to make laws and set up courts for the whole district. The patent also exempted them from taxation for seven years.

Acting on this authority, the tiny towns of the Monmouth

region sent deputies to an assembly meeting in Shrewsbury on December 12, 1667. They continued to hold their own independent assembly for a number of years. These assemblies passed laws, dealt out justice, and set rules under which land could be bought and sold.

What this meant was that the towns of the Monmouth district were acting like an independent colony. They could not help but come in conflict with the government. In the proprietors' view, only Berkeley and Carteret could dispose of the land; only *they* could run the affairs of the entire colony, with the assistance of the general assembly for which they had provided.

With Governor Philip Carteret presiding, this first general assembly met at Elizabethtown on May 29, 1668. There were eleven delegates present from the towns of Bergen, Elizabethtown, Woodbridge, Newark, Middletown and Shrewsbury. The legislative session lasted for just four days. The delegates concentrated on adopting a penal code so stern that Philip Carteret must have been surprised at some of its provisions.

The death penalty was prescribed for a long list of crimes: murder, arson, perjury, kidnapping, witchcraft, treason, burglary in some cases—and even for the smiting or cursing of parents by their children. For lying, the offender was to be fined or placed in the stocks. For the "beastly vice of drunkeness," he was to be fined or lashed or put in the stocks.

Gambling and lighthearted diversions of all kinds were frowned on. "All prizes, stage plays, games, marques, revels, bull-baiting and cock-fighting, which excite people to rudeness, cruelty, looseness and irreligion" were to be discouraged and punished by the courts. Violation of the Sabbath by doing house work, unnecessary traveling, or amusing oneself was to be punished by fines, a time in the stocks, imprisonment or whipping.

Having set such a strict code, this first general assembly broke up, and its deputies hurried back to work on their farms. They had, however, done more than they knew. They had laid the groundwork for one of the first outbreaks of rebellion in the American colonies.

The dispute involved the Monmouth region. The two deputies from Monmouth, James Glover and John Bowne, had been among the original Monmouth settlers and were supposed to be men of high standing in their communities. At the Elizabethtown assembly, however, they had taken the required oath of loyalty to the King and the proprietors —an act that shocked their independent-minded voters back home. The Quakers, of course, were opposed to all such oaths as a matter of principle.

But more than principle was involved here. The Monmouth settlers were aware that the proprietors' land claims might threaten their titles to their homesteads. In addition they treasured the pledge in their patent that they should not be taxed for seven years. And so anger swept the Monmouth area because Glover and Bowne, by taking the oath, had placed these precious rights in danger.

Town meetings were held in the Monmouth district, and the actions of the two deputies were objected to and denounced. The claim was made that they had not had enough votes to be elected and so should never have been seated in the assembly. Basing their stand on this ground the Monmouth towns announced that they would refuse to be bound by anything that Glover and Bowne had done.

They went further. They offered to send other delegates, properly elected, to the next asembly—but only on certain conditions. The new deputies would not be permitted to take the oath of allegiance to the proprietors unless the proprietors agreed in advance to recognize all the rights the settlers had been granted under the Nicolls' patent.

The making of such conditions carried with it the clear threat of rebellion. When the delegates from Monmouth's Middletown and Shrewsbury districts appeared for the next meeting of the assembly in November, 1668, they were not permitted to take their seats.

Middletown and Shrewsbury answered by announcing that they would pay no taxes levied by the assembly—and they named Nicolls' seven-year tax-exemption clause in justification. They carried their rebellion further. They proclaimed that, if any attempt was made to seize their cattle or goods by tax collectors, they would resist.

To justify their stand, the Middletowners now held a town meeting and drew up a document giving their views of the matter. They protested that they did not understand what proprietary government meant. The King's writs they understood. But writs in the name of the lord proprietor were something such as "we simple creatures never heard of before." How, they asked, could Governor Carteret say that their patent was of no account, that the deeds they held by purchase from the Indians with the approval of Nicolls were worthless, that their lands really belong to the proprietors? How could the governor and his council prevent them from electing their own town officials or say that, if they did, they would be "proceeded against as mutineers"?

The lords proprietors seemed to be demanding absolute ownership of all property and absolute rule in the colony. This would make the people "absolute tenants" forever and ever. If they took the oath and paid their quit rents, they would bind themselves to a lasting obedience that "would be a dishonor to him that gave it." This, they refused to do. They would insist on the privileges and freedoms guaranteed them by Nicolls. They would insist on making their own laws. They were willing to cooperate and offer obedience on larger matters that lay outside this grant of rights, but more they would not do. And they were determined, "with the assistance of God," to stick up for their rights and their patent.

It was unmistakable defiance. Here clearly stated for the first time in colonial America was the issue that was to lead to the Revolution: popular rule versus absentee rule.

In this case it was rule by the proprietors, but finally by the King. These freedom-breathing, independent settlers were going to insist on making their own laws, levying their own taxes. Any attempt by a foreign power, whether the proprietors or the King, to force upon them taxes and rules not of their own making would provoke fierce and instant rebellion.

The issue, though first taken up by the Monmouth settlers, affected the lives of almost everyone in New Jersey. The Elizabethtown Associates—and all the settlements that had been spun off from this great grant of land—rested their claims upon purchase from the Indians and the patent by Nicolls. If these were not good, then nobody could truly say that he owned his homestead. Soon the whole colony was up in arms.

Twice in 1672, delegates from Elizabethtown, Newark, Woodbridge, Piscataway and Bergen held their own assemblies. These meetings had no legal status. Governor Philip Carteret and his council had not called them and refused to have anything to do with them. And so, at the first session, the delegates talked a lot about "the safety of the country," and then disbanded, having accomplished nothing.

But at the second meeting on May 14, 1672, they found a colorful way to express their defiance in a deed that could not be ignored. Another Carteret had come to Elizabethtown. He was Captain James Carteret, said to be an illegitimate son of Sir George. Captain James was on his way to the Carolinas, but having been given some messages to Governor Philip Carteret, he stopped over at Elizabethtown.

Just what happened between the two Carterets was never

clear. But James obviously disliked Philip, whom he later accused of bungling and mismanagement. The settlers, hearing of the feud, now invented a master stroke.

They called a meeting of the assembly at Elizabethtown. Governor Philip Carteret ignored them as he had before. But this time the settlers had an answer for the governor. They elected Captain James Carteret "President" of the assembly. They also proclaimed that he was "President of the Country." In effect, they set up their own government in defiance of the proprietors.

James Carteret played along with the people. He announced that he had a warrant from his father to rule (which he certainly did not have), and he proclaimed himself "President." Governor Philip denounced the whole thing and promised to reward those who backed him and the proprietors. But there were not many settlers in New Jersey who could be lured by these promises. Public affairs were in chaos, with two different governments claiming the right to rule.

There was only one solution. Philip Carteret and his councillors decided that he would have to go to London to lay the dispute before Lord Berkeley and Sir George Carteret. Philip named John Berry as deputy governor to rule in his absence, though Berry actually could accomplish nothing. In early July, Philip Carteret and three of his councillors sailed for England.

Sir George Carteret was at this time an aging man of seventy-two, and he and Lord Berkeley had had more headaches than profit from the princely land grant made to them by the Duke of York so many years before. This latest trouble made them angry and impatient. Sir George was enraged at the mischief-making of his son, Captain James. He issued an order denouncing James for his conduct and ordering him to get out of New Jersey.

The proprietors then went further. They took up the whole matter with their patron, the Duke of York. The Duke issued an order holding that the Nicolls land grants were worthless. He informed the New Jersey rebels that they had no right to their lands unless they had acquired them from the proprietors. And the proprietors promptly issued a decree. It stated that no one could hold land or take part in the running of the government who had not obtained a deed from them and paid his annual quit rent.

These orders amounted to a complete and disastrous defeat for the New Jersey rebels. Just how they would have been received in time—whether they would have been accepted or defied—remains a matter of question, for just at this point an event took place that changed everything.

England was again at war with Holland. The Dutch were hardy and skillful seamen, and as soon as the fighting started, they sent a fleet to attack the British colonies in the New World. They found New York as poorly prepared for defense under the English as it had been under Peter Stuyvesant when the English came. On August 8, 1673, some six hundred Dutch soldiers landed on Manhattan Island at a point near what is now Wall Street and marched against Fort James. The British surrendered as meekly as the Dutch had done, and all the Hudson River towns, all the settlements in New Jersey also surrendered and came once more under Dutch control.

The Dutch kept careful records, and from these we can judge how small the population of New Jersey was at the time. Elizabethtown had 80 people in it; Newark, 86; Woodbridge, 54; Piscataway, 43; Middletown, 60; and Shrewsbury 68, of whom 18 were Quakers. Most of these residents took the oath of allegiance to the Dutch, and a Dutch governor-general was appointed to rule both New York and New Jersey.

His reign was brief. By the Treaty of Westminster, signed in February, 1674, the Dutch gave up New York and New Jersey, and the English once more controlled the two colonies.

The brief return of Dutch rule, however, had changed many things. It had wiped out the rights of the old owners. It had created a new situation.

English authorities recognized this, and King Charles made a new gift of New Jersey to the Duke of York. And the Duke made out new papers, once more giving New Jersey to Berkeley and Carteret.

Berkeley was by this time very unhappy with the whole business. And so, on March 18, 1674, he sold his half of

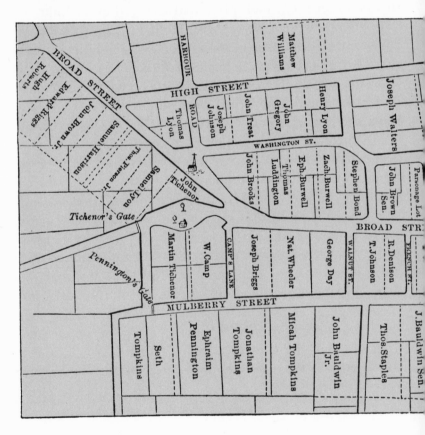

New Jersey—the southern and western half—to John Fenwick. Fenwick, it appears, was acting for a fellow Quaker, Edward Byllinge. Byllinge, in turn, drew other Quakers into the enterprise. These included William Penn, the founder of Pennsylvania.

This left Sir George Carteret as the sole proprietor of the eastern and northern half of New Jersey—all that part of the region above a diagonal line beginning at Little Egg Harbor on the coast and running to the vicinity of the Delaware Water Gap. This area, called East Jersey, was the only really settled part of the colony. Nearly all of West Jersey

A plan of Newark as it was laid out by the original settlers

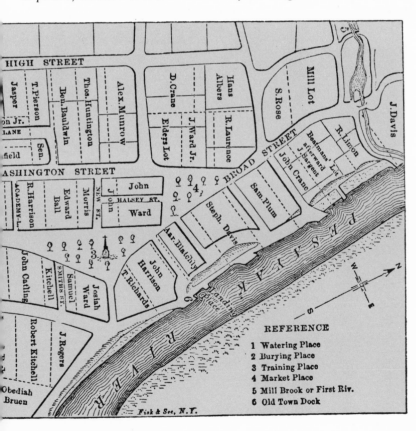

REFERENCE

1 Watering Place
2 Burying Place
3 Training Place
4 Market Place
5 Mill Brook or First Riv.
6 Old Town Dock

was still an unbroken wilderness, with a few Dutch settlers around Burlington and a few homesteads in clearings along the lower Delaware.

The brief Dutch rule led to one other important change. The Duke of York was determined to try to bring some order to his unruly colonies overseas, and so he named a single governor to have power over all the land "from ye West side of Connecticut River to ye East Side of Delaware Bay."

Unfortunately, the man to whom the Duke gave powers "of the most arbitrary nature" was a man who loved power too well—and so misused it. He was Major Edmund Andros, who was to become one of the most hated governors in colonial history.

five

Governor
Arrests Governor

Edmund Andros liked to arrest people—even other governors. And the confused situation in New Jersey gave him plenty of opportunity to satisfy his thirst.

New Jersey was kept in a constant boil of trouble. A large part of it resulted from the fact that authorities in England could never do one clear, simple thing. They always had to do at least two things at the same time, or at about the same time, and one was always certain to conflict with the other.

The appointment of Andros as governor of Connecticut, New York and New Jersey was a perfect example. The Duke of York himself ordered Andros to govern this whole vast region. But the Duke seems not to have considered that he had also renewed his gift of New Jersey to Berkeley and Carteret. *They* believed they could go ahead as before and run their own government. So there were soon two governors trying to rule the same colony, and there was bound to be trouble.

Added to this confusion and conflict was new trouble in West Jersey. This stemmed from the sale of this part of the colony by Berkeley to John Fenwick.

Fenwick was a peppery major who had served under Oliver Cromwell in the English civil war. He had been selected by Cromwell to be in charge of an honor guard at the execution of King Charles I on January 30, 1648, a sign that he must have fought well.

Fenwick's father had sat in Parliament under Cromwell. Fenwick, by inheritance and marriage, was the owner of large estates in Berkshire. After the restoration of King Charles II, he left the army and occupied himself with the management of his estates, keeping an exact record of every penny received and every penny spent. He also at this time fell under the influence of William Penn and became a Quaker. His devotion to his new Quaker faith led to his being twice jailed and fined in England, once in 1666 and again in 1670. These experiences as well as the influence of Penn turned his thoughts to America.

As a result, when Lord Berkeley decided to dispose of

Lord John Berkeley sold his holdings in West Jersey in 1674

his West Jersey holdings in 1674, Fenwick bought them. It might seem that this should have been a simple matter— but it wasn't.

Fenwick, though he owned broad acres in England, seems to have been short of the kind of ready cash needed to start a settlement in the New World. To raise money and settle his debts, he parted with nine-tenths of West Jersey to Edward Byllinge, another Quaker. And Byllinge, also having financial troubles, brought in another group of Quakers, including William Penn.

This new Quaker ownership quickly became unhappy about Fenwick's ownership of one-tenth of West Jersey. There was no question that he had kept one-tenth for himself. But *which* one-tenth? On this there was no agreement, and so the seeds were laid for endless trouble for Fenwick.

Fenwick had a clear idea of which one-tenth he owned. In the spring of 1675, he sailed to take possession of it. With him on the ship *Griffin* went his three daughters by his first wife and the husbands of two of them. His second wife, Mary, who seems to have had considerable money of her own, preferred the comforts of England, stayed home—and was never to see him again.

Fenwick, his family and his servants landed in southern New Jersey on June 23, 1675. Fenwick named the place Salem—taken from a Hebrew word meaning "peace"—and promptly set about laying out a town. Perhaps it is some indication of Fenwick's high standing in England that other ships swiftly followed, bringing more Quaker families to swell the size of the settlement.

From the first, Fenwick dealt wisely with the Indians. He entered into a treaty with them by which he purchased all of their lands from Old Man's Creek to the Morris River. In all the history of the Fenwick settlement, there was never an instance of an Indian being killed by a white man—or a white man by an Indian.

John Fenwick built Ivy Point for himself and his daughters

Fenwick built himself a home at Ivy Point in Salem, laid out lots and farms for settlers in Salem and Greenwich, and appeared on the way to prosperity. But now the old troubles about which part of West Jersey he owned rose in England to plague him.

The Quakers who had been brought into the deal by Byllinge started legal action, trying to get Fenwick's property. They obtained a court order that said he could not sell any land without their consent. A copy of this order was sent to Governor Andros in New York, reaching him December 5, 1675. By this time, Fenwick had already sold off some lots in Salem and Greenwich. He was selling others, and soon between eighty and one hundred homes would be built on the disputed property.

Fenwick ignored Andros' order to stop his land sales. He argued that he was the sole owner of the Salem region, having bought all Lord Berkeley's rights, and that he could set up his own government there.

Fenwick was having his own troubles in his colony, however. When lots were drawn for farm acreage outside the town, Richard Noble drew section No. 4, but he was unhappy with it and refused to accept it. Apparently, too, representatives of the Quaker group seeking Fenwick's property drifted into Salem and caused trouble.

Fenwick himself later wrote that "my person has been several times assaulted, my life often and greatly endangered by forceing [*sic*] a gun, laden with many swan shot, within four yards of my breast, and a pistol discharged, with two bullets, within two or three feet of my neck. . . ."

In November, 1676, Andros ordered Fenwick to give himself up in New York, but Fenwick refused. Andros was not a man to be stopped. Fitting out an armed expedition, he sent his soldiers to Salem with orders to take Fenwick "dead or alive." Fenwick later described what happened on the night of December 8, 1676, while he was sleeping:

"My house was beset, my door broken down, and my person seized in the night time by armed men sent to execute a paper order from the Governor of New York, to whom I was sent a prisoner in the depth of winter by sea. . . ."

Andros kept Fenwick in prison, off and on, for two years. He presided at Fenwick's trial, and finally had to release him because, as Fenwick wrote, "it was not, nor could be proved, that I had broken any of the King's laws."

In 1682 an agreement was reached with the Quaker interests. Fenwick was allowed to keep 150,000 acres in the Salem-Greenwich area he had colonized, and he signed the rest of the tract he had claimed over to William Penn. When he died in December, 1683, at the age of sixty-five, he made Penn executor of his estate, and Penn went ahead with the development of Greenwich.

In the meantime, the Quakers had founded other settlements in West Jersey. In September, 1677, the ship *Kent* with two hundred and thirty passengers entered the Delaware and went upstream to Burlington, where the Quakers landed and developed the town that was to become the capital of West Jersey. In late 1677 and 1678 more shiploads of Quaker settlers arrived and took up land along the Delaware below Burlington. In New York, Governor Andros watched all this, and though he claimed to govern New Jersey, he did not interfere. Perhaps he had no wish to tangle with the powerful William Penn.

No such consideration stayed his hand where East Jersey was concerned. There Sir George Carteret had once more named Philip Carteret governor. Andros and Carteret had crossed the Atlantic on the same ship, reaching New York at the end of October, 1674. There appears to have been no conflict between these fellow passengers at this time. Andros apparently did not advance any claim that he, not Carteret, should govern in New Jersey.

Philip Carteret went on to Elizabethtown and picked up the reins of government. He called his council together, and in December he issued a stern proclamation.

He declared that no land title was good unless it had been obtained from the proprietors. Quit rents must be paid. Those that had not been paid since 1670 would be collected in addition to the current rental. If the settlers refused, their goods and cattle would be seized in payment.

Furthermore, Philip Carteret denounced the land riots that had occurred before the Dutch conquest. He accused his riotous people of having surrendered quickly to the Dutch because they hoped to escape "the hand of justice by inviteing [*sic*] an enemy to protect them."

Many of the settlers now yielded. A number of residents

in Elizabethtown and Newark applied for surveys of their lands and purchased deeds from the proprietors to protect their holdings. Carteret seemed in firm control, and the land riots appeared to be things of the past.

But, at this point, Edmund Andros chose to meddle. For nearly three years, he had made no claim to rule in New Jersey. In fact, he appeared to be on friendly terms with Carteret, and he even visited Carteret's home and dined with him before sailing on a brief trip to England.

He returned in August, 1678, a more conceited and impossible man. He had been knighted, and he was now Sir Edmund Andros. Records of the time make it clear that he had done much talking with the Duke of York's advisers at court. Many of these felt that the Duke had made a mistake in giving New Jersey to Berkeley and Carteret. They were anxious to see him regain control of the colony. It seems that they probably pushed Andros to use his authority—and Andros was a man who needed little pushing. He returned to America prepared to act. And Philip Carteret obliged by giving him a perfect excuse.

In 1679 Carteret announced that New Jersey ships trading with the West Indies did not have to pass through the port of New York and pay customs duties there. They could sail and return directly to Perth Amboy at the mouth of the Raritan River. The New Jersey settlers had long wanted to make Perth Amboy a rival to the port of New York.

Andros' reaction was swift. On March 8, 1679, he sent Carteret a court order to stop governing in New Jersey. Andros also said that a beacon and fort were needed at Sandy Hook—the long sand spit that stretches from the Jersey shore out toward the entrance of New York harbor —and that he intended to build these structures. Finally, going over Carteret's head, he advised New Jersey settlers not to obey Carteret's "illegal" rule.

Here was the making of a confused tangle. Carteret at once argued with Andros. Carteret said he was acting "by their Sovereign's positive orders." If Andros tried to build a fort at Sandy Hook, he would resist. If Andros tried to use force, there would be war. Carteret concluded that "if any Blood be shed, it will be contrary to our desires, and the just and righteous God require it at your Hands, who are the Causes thereof."

Andros reacted to this defiance by calling an assembly meeting at Woodbridge on April 7, 1679. Carteret ordered the assembly delegates to ignore the call. He told Andros that if he sent further messengers into the colony, they would be seized and treated as "spies and disturbers of the peace."

Ignoring this, Andros and his aides set out for Elizabethtown on April 5. At the shore they were met by Carteret, backed by a small army of armed men. For a moment, the two hostile forces faced each other, and battle appeared certain. But then Andros adopted a friendly tone. He had come in peace, he said, and all he wanted was to be allowed to talk to the settlers. This, Carteret permitted. Andros denounced Carteret's rule, seemingly with little effect. He then went to Carteret's house, dined with him, and finally departed for New York. It seemed that he had failed, but Andros was not the man to accept defeat.

On May 1, he signed an order for Philip Carteret's arrest. As he had in the case of Fenwick, he dispatched a posse of soldiers quietly to Elizabethtown. They surprised Carteret without his armed guard and apparently handled him with unnecessary roughness, for he later wrote that he was "so disabled by Bruises and Hurts that I fear I shall hardly be a perfect man again."

In this shape, Philip Carteret was hauled off to New York, where he was imprisoned until May 27. Then he was brought to trail, charged with constantly and riotously try-

Andros' men surprised Carteret and hauled him off to imprisonment in New York

ing to govern New Jersey in defiance of the Duke of York's orders.

Carteret defended himself strongly. He attacked the fact that Andros, his accuser, also sat as judge at the trial to determine his fate. This argument apparently appealed to the New York jury as just, for the jurors returned a verdict of not guilty.

Andros, in a rage, refused to accept their decision and sent them out to consider the error of their ways, demanding that they convict. They went, reconsidered, and returned with another verdict—just like the first, not guilty.

Andros was forced to free Carteret, but made him promise not to try to govern in New Jersey. Andros and his council then sailed to Elizabethtown to meet the New Jersey assembly and take over the government. But they found themselves face to face with a group of stiff-necked colonists.

The assembly wanted Andros' promise to call it into regular session every October. Andros refused. He would call assembly meetings only when he thought necessary, he said. Speaker John Bowne debated the point for two hours, arguing for the rights of the people, but Andros refused to budge.

An explanation of Andros' conduct in the following months may be found in the fact that he possessed a bit of secret knowledge. He knew that Sir George Carteret had died in England at the age of eighty. He evidently reasoned that, with this death, the Carteret family would lose its influence at court. Hence he could do very much as he pleased.

Lady Elizabeth Carteret used her influence at court to get Andros recalled

What pleased him, however, did not please his New Jersey subjects. They were angry and rebellious, and they didn't hesitate to make their feelings known. One, William Taylor, denounced Andros to all the men in an ordinary (the term applied to a tavern in those days). Andros, he said, was "a rogue and a traitor, and he had treacherously imprisoned Philip Carteret." Taylor was arrested and hauled off to New York, where Andros forced him to apologize and promise to behave himself.

Woodbridge rebelled against Andros' rule in July, 1680. Andros had insisted only he could approve local magistrates nominated by the townspeople. The Woodbridge citizens argued that their patent gave them the right to name their own. They refused to submit any names to Andros for his consideration. Samuel Moore, who signed this notice of defiance, was arrested, brought before Andros, lectured and finally released because of his "mean condition, many children, &."

These and similar incidents had the colony in an uproar. Word of Andros' conduct was sent back to England. There it became clear the New York governor had made one great mistake. The Carterets had not lost all their influence at court. Lady Elizabeth Carteret, the widow, got the ear of the Duke of York, and at the end of 1680 Andros was recalled.

In New Jersey, Philip Carteret again proclaimed himself governor. The Duke of York, he said, had denied any knowledge of Andros' "illegal" acts in "usurping the government of New Jersey."

The Carteret rule, however, was now coming to an end. In the settlement of Sir George's estate, Lady Carteret sold East Jersey to a group of Quakers headed by William Penn. This meant that the Quakers now owned both East and West Jersey. They set up their own government for the colony under a board of twenty-four proprietors.

six

The First Revolution

East Jersey and West Jersey developed as two separate colonies. East Jersey was a mixture of many nationalities and religious faiths. West Jersey was largely inhabited by Quakers. East Jersey was forever in turmoil, riot following riot, rebellion following rebellion. West Jersey was largely quiet and peaceable, with few disturbances. East Jersey was the home of little people, fiercely democratic, handling their own local affairs in town meetings. West Jersey became the home of the large landowner, developing a plantation system much like that of Virginia and Maryland.

A major reason for these contrasts, though not the only one, may be found in the different strength of the Quaker influence in the two sections and the different motives of the Quaker proprietors. In West Jersey, the Quakers came to settle and make the land their own. In East Jersey, which they bought from the Carteret estate, they recognized that New England influences were so strong they could never change them. East Jersey was for them a moneymaking adventure. And they could make money only through the sale of vast acres of wild lands and the collection of the much-hated quit rents.

Here was the underlying cause for the slow building of a spirit of rebellion. It was a rebellion so fierce that it became known in colonial days as "the revolution."

Like everything else in New Jersey history, the affairs of of government during this period when rebellion was forming were greatly confused. After the death of King Charles II in May, 1685, his brother, the Duke of York, became King. He was known as James II, and he had one firm resolve: to strengthen his power in the colonies, wiping out as far as possible all traces of popular government.

To do this, he started court actions to cancel the charters of East Jersey, West Jersey, Delaware, Connecticut and Rhode Island. He directed that all of these colonies be combined under one official, the governor of New York, and he appointed the already much-disliked Sir Edmund Andros to this post. Andros returned to New York in August, 1688, and started acting like a kind of subking.

The East Jersey proprietors were alarmed by this change. They did not want their territory joined to New York, and they protested to the king that they held clear title from the Carterets and the Indians. They protested, too—an argument that was to be repeated again and again until the Revolution of 1776—that they should not be subjected to taxes levied by the government of New York, a foreign legislature in which they were not represented. They prayed that the King would combine East Jersey and West Jersey and select a governor, chosen from among the proprietors, to rule the combined colony.

James II was determined, however, to assert his royal rule, and the Jerseys were annexed to New York. A compromise of sorts was worked out by which a deputy gov-

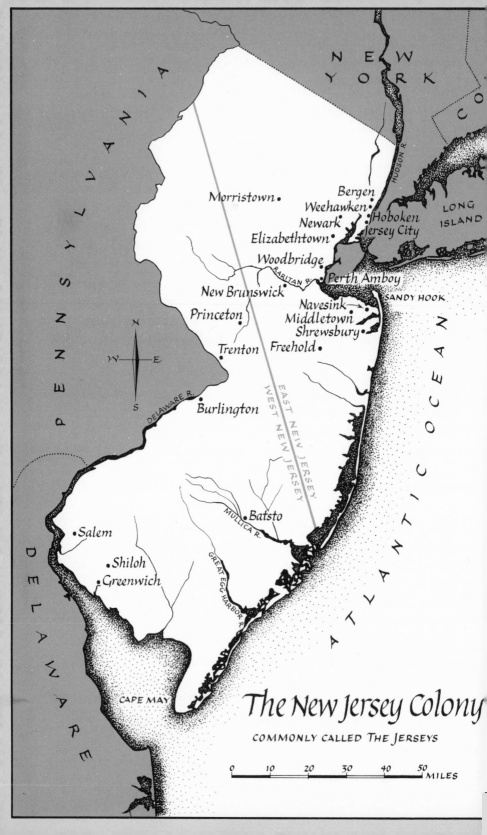

The New Jersey Colony

COMMONLY CALLED THE JERSEYS

ernor, chosen from the ranks of the proprietors, was named to have direct charge of New Jersey affairs. The man selected for this task was Andrew Hamilton. He served as a kind of half-governor, the proprietors' man in New Jersey, subject always to being overruled by the royal governor in New York—and so often in conflict with him.

The confusion and the conflict helped to undermine all government, of whatever kind. Andros' term in office in New York was brief, but the real problem was that there was not one clear line of authority. Two officials were trying to do the job one should have done. When they quarreled with each other, the colonists did very much as they pleased.

The authority that the proprietors had had in the days of the Carterets seemed to have all but vanished. There were many temptations to ignore the weak rule that existed.

New Jersey still had many acres of wild land, there for the taking. Many squatters went into the woods and fields, carving out for themselves homesteads of their own without paying too much attention to the property rights of the proprietors. They often claimed, when questioned, that they had purchased their lands from the "real" owners, the Indians. If they needed further support, they brought up the old argument that the original Elizabethtown-Nicolls grant was the real basis for a title—that the Carterets and their successors didn't have proper claim to the land anyway.

The new Quaker proprietors of East Jersey, wanting to make money out of their investment, instructed Governor Hamilton to stop the land-squatting and force payment for legal titles. He was also to collect the quit rents. Hamilton appointed a collector to determine how much in back rents was due and to bring suit against those who had not paid or who refused to pay. This attempt to collect the land rents stirred up all the old hatreds.

One famous lawsuit of the time shows just how bitter and important was the issue. In early 1693 a man named James Fullerton received title to a tract on the Delaware from the proprietors. He had begun to clear it when another man named Jeffry Jones ordered him to stop. Jones claimed the acreage was his under the original Elizabethtown-Nicolls patent, and he drove Fullerton off "with force and arms." Fullerton sued in the courts.

The case was heard before a New Jersey jury. The jury decided for Jones, in effect upholding the lawfulness of the Nicolls patent claims. The judge, appointed by the proprietors through their governor, then held that the verdict was against the weight of the evidence. He threw out the jury's decision and ruled that the land properly belonged to the proprietors' man, Fullerton.

Jones now appealed, and the case was fought all the way up to the King's Privy Council in London. The Privy Council again reversed things. It ordered the judge's verdict in favor of Fullerton thrown out. So Jones became the winner, and this highest of high decisions appeared at the moment to settle the issue. According to this, the Nicolls land claims were good, and the proprietors really had no right to large sections of New Jersey that they claimed.

The decision was like a spark applied to a powder keg. The Elizabethtown faction claimed that the Fullerton-Jones case proved two things: 1. that the proprietors had no legal right to lands they claimed—and so no authority to govern— and 2. that the people of the colony could not expect justice from the proprietors' hand-picked governors and judges.

The result was the outbreak of disturbances called "the revolution." The settlers around Middletown, always an independent and unruly lot, were in revolt. They refused to pay quit rents. They refused to recognize that the proprietors had any authority over them.

Governor Andrew Hamilton, trying to restore order, named Lewis Morris as his deputy to put down what amounted to armed rebellion. Morris thundered, according to an account of the time, that "if any man resisted him, he would spill his blood." To show how tough he could be, he ordered the Sheriff to arrest one Richard Saltar, a leading troublemaker. But when the Sheriff tried to make the arrest, Saltar's followers seized *him*, "banged him, broke his head and sent him packing." Not long afterward, Morris and the forces of law met face to face with a small army of about one hundred armed Middletown settlers. A pitched battle was avoided only by the retreat of the law men.

Even more sensational was the affair of the famous pirate. Word got around Middletown that a local sailor, Moses Butterworth, had sailed with the notorious Captain Kidd. Kidd was a legally commissioned privateersman of the day who had turned pirate and raided far and wide. He was popularly supposed to have buried hoards of treasure along the New Jersey and Long Island coasts, though no trace of such treasure was ever found. Kidd himself was hanged at Execution Dock in London, and word that Butterworth had been one of his pirate followers naturally caused quite a sensation in Middletown.

Butterworth was arrested and is said to have confessed that he had indeed sailed with Captain Kidd. His trial was set for March 25, 1701. Governor Hamilton and four of his councillors, including Morris, traveled to Middletown to preside at the trial.

The trial had hardly started when a Middletowner in the audience, one Samuel Willet, leaped up and cried out that the officials lacked any authority to hold court and that he was going to break it up. Running outside, he made a speech to a number of militiamen who were drilling on the village green. The militia, not liking the governor and his aides any more than Willet did, joined forces with him, burst into the courtroom and rescued Butterworth.

In the free-for-all with the forces of the law, however, two of the Middletown ringleaders, Richard and Benjamin Borden, were wounded. One of them (accounts of the day do not say which one) was hurt so badly that it was thought he might die. This so enraged the Middletowners that they seized the governor and all his councillors and threw them into prison. If Borden died, they threatened, they would hang the governor in revenge.

Fortunately, Borden lived, and Governor Hamilton, Morris and the other councillors were freed—and were no doubt glad to get out of Middletown with their lives.

It was clear to the more sober and responsible colonists that this state of affairs could not be allowed to continue. New Jersey was becoming a lawless land in which no man's life and property were safe. And so the Elizabethtown group took a step it had formerly opposed. It petitioned the King to unite New Jersey and New York under one royal governor, abolishing proprietary rule.

In England, by this time, there had been many changes. King James II had been forced off the throne and had been succeeded by William and Mary. And now, in the spring of 1702, just at the time the New Jersey troubles were coming to a head, there was a new monarch—Queen Anne.

The Queen, in one of her first acts, granted the plea of the New Jerseyans. The rights of the proprietors through the land grants dating back to the time when James was Duke of York were upheld. But it was now also held that this was all the proprietors had ever been given in the first place —the land. They had never had any right to appoint their own governors or set up their own government. Government was the business of the Crown.

On April 17, 1702, Queen Anne named her own cousin,

Edward Hyde, Lord Cornbury, to govern both New York and New Jersey. He was to be the only governor of New Jersey, and his authority was clear and unquestioned.

All the evidence of the time would seem to indicate that New Jerseyans breathed a great sigh of relief. They were tired of the excesses and violence of their own "revolution," and they looked forward to a settled life under royal rule.

But they could not know what the future would bring. They had not yet met Lord Cornbury.

seven

The Cornbury Scandal

It was clear from the start that New Jersey had lost many of its privileges when it sought the protection and security of government by the Crown. Some idea of the nature of the change may be seen by comparing some of the rules of the government of West Jersey with the rules of the new order.

When William Penn and the Quakers settled West Jersey, they issued a document known as Concessions and Agreements—a grant of liberties so broad that it is often described as the forerunner of the Bill of Rights.

Absolute religious freedom was guaranteed to all faiths. Freedom of speech was pledged. The governing body was to be a board of commissioners elected by the people. Local justices and constables were to be chosen by the people, and the people's legislature was to fix the number of the higher courts, their officers and salaries. Trial by a jury composed of "Twelve good and lawful Men of his Neighborhood" was guaranteed to anyone accused of crime.

Things changed when the Crown took over the administration of both East and West Jersey in 1702. The right to vote was greatly limited. A man could cast a ballot only if he owned one hundred acres of land. No one could sit in the assembly who owned fewer than one thousand acres. These provisions, it was thought, would reduce the power of "the rabble" responsible for the recent riots.

Power was concentrated in the hands of the royal governor and his hand-picked council. Appointments of law and judicial officers were in the governor's hands. He alone could call the assembly into session, and if he did not call, it did not meet. Just one major power had been reserved for the people, and this was to prove more important than all the others. Only the assembly could levy taxes for the public defense and the support of the colonial government. Even the governor could not be paid unless the assembly voted him the funds.

So the scene was set for a tug-of-war between the royal governor and the people. And Lord Cornbury was just the man to make sure that this clash would be as fierce and bitter as possible.

His rule began with a typically disgraceful event. The power of the new Quaker rulers of East Jersey had become centered in what was known as the Scotch faction. When the Quakers bought this half of Jersey to make money, some important and powerful members of their new board of proprietors were Scotsmen who came and settled around Perth Amboy. This Raritan River port quickly became known as the stronghold of the wealthier, proprietary interests, while Elizabethtown remained the headquarters of the common people.

Just how the Perth Amboy Scotch groups understood Lord Cornbury so quickly was never disclosed. But the event showed they knew their man. The new governor and cousin of the Queen had hardly arrived in New York when a couple of representatives of the Scotch paid him a visit. When they departed, Lord Cornbury had been enriched by some two hundred British pounds, a large sum of money in those days.

The effect of this bribe was soon seen. Cornbury named Sheriff Thomas Gordon, of the Scotch faction, to conduct the election for members of the assembly. The Elizabeth-town-Nicolls patent group turned out nearly four hundred voters; the proprietary party, only forty-two. But the Sheriff ruled that the four hundred had "lost" the election, the forty-two had "won," and all the delegates he passed on were members of the Scotch proprietary party.

It might seem that there should now have been a meeting of minds between the bought-governor and the assembly he had helped to seat. However, few things in life are more certain than this: the payment of a bribe does not lay the basis for great trust. The proprietary faction had succeeded in keeping their opponents out of the assembly. But they put no great faith in the governor who had accepted their cash, perhaps reasoning that a man who is for sale is also for sale to a higher bidder.

When the assembly met in November, 1703, therefore, there was bickering and dispute instead of harmony. Cornbury wanted a tax measure passed. Government bills had been gathering since 1699 and needed to be paid; besides, he wanted a salary for himself. The assembly, realizing that its hold on the purse strings was the only power it had, wanted to wring a number of concessions out of the governor first. Cornbury refused to be wrung. He signed one minor bill, then dismissed the assembly. Nothing had been accomplished.

A year later almost the same scene was repeated. This time, the assembly dangled a bit of bait under Lord Cornbury's nose. It offered to grant 1,500 pounds for governmental expenses the first year, 1,000 for the second. But it held off in passing the bill until it got from the governor certain concessions that it wanted.

Cornbury would give nothing. He was not in need of money now. The New York legislature had granted him a salary for seven years. It had also given him full power to dispose of huge tracts of wilderness land—a grant that meant fortunes in land-dealing for what became known as "the Cornbury ring." The result was that the New Jersey assembly had lost its bargaining power, and Cornbury, not needing it, could act as high-handed as he pleased.

Now the Elizabethtown-Nicolls faction heard of the bribe that had been paid to Cornbury by the proprietary party. They decided to buy the governor for themselves by raising the price. Richard Saltar and John Bowne went around the the countryside collecting what was called a "blind tax." The people were told only that the money was to be used to get rid of the hated quit rents on their land—and that it was to be "for the good of the country."

No one knows just how much money was raised. Later estimates ranged from 800 to 1,500 pounds. Anyway, it was a bribe fit for a king. With this booty in their pockets, Saltar and Bowne visited Cornbury's office in New York. They did not see the governor himself, but they left their offering in care of a trusted underling. And, as they later said, there was "all the reason in ye World to believe his Lordship had it."

This payment set the stage for a great storm. Cornbury promptly switched sides. When the proprietary party kept control of the assembly by a couple of votes in a new election, the governor himself disqualified three Quakers on the ground they didn't own enough property to qualify for their seats. This gave control to the anti-proprietary faction with whom Cornbury was now doing business.

With the assembly and the governor working together, a number of laws were now passed, most of them so unwise that they could not fail to enrage a good part of the people. For example, there was a severe Militia Act. This provided that all males from sixteen to sixty must muster for training four times a year or pay a fine of one pound for failure to do so. The act infuriated the Quakers, who were opposed to bearing arms in any circumstances. If they also refused to pay the fine, as expected, the act provided that their goods and property could be seized in payment—a provision that pleased the members of the greedy "Cornbury ring."

The Elizabethtown-Nicolls faction, which had raised Cornbury's bribe price through the "blind tax," got several things it wanted. A law was passed abolishing the requirement that a man must own one hundred acres of land to vote. Instead, he needed only "a freehold," a general term meaning merely the possession of some property. A tax measure was also passed to raise revenue for the government, and this provided that taxes should be paid on *all* lands. This was aimed directly at the proprietary interests which had been paying no taxes on the vast, undeveloped acres they were holding for sale.

As a reward to Cornbury for cooperating in all this, the assembly voted him the princely salary of 2,000 pounds a year for two years. Even this wasn't enough for Cornbury. He approved bills for more money than had been voted, seeming to assume the assembly would have to pay them some day.

The costs of this program were staggering, compared with what the colonists had paid before. The poorer people as well as the wealthy were outraged. In a day when hard money was scarce for most, and payment of bills was often made in the form of farm produce or goods, many citizens had no way of raising the money necessary to pay their taxes. Some were able to borrow, but many more, who had no credit, were in a sorry plight. "Very many there was that sold milch Cowes to raise six shillings," says one account.

The Scotch proprietors, victims of so much of the legislation, protested angrily to authorities in England against Cornbury's conduct. And the common people, so often at odds with the proprietors, were themselves so badly hurt that they joined the wealthy in revolt. In 1706 Cornbury could not even get enough delegates to come to the assembly to hold a session. And in 1707, when the assembly did consent to meet, it would have been better for the Governor if it had not.

Cornbury wanted the assembly to extend the Militia Act and to grant him another 1,500 pounds. Instead, the assembly began an investigation of the "blind tax" scandal. When it dragged out into the light of day the whole business about the Cornbury bribe, Bowne was expelled from his seat in the assembly, and Saltar fled to Pennsylvania. The assembly then refused to vote any new taxes and drew up a list of grievances, one dealing specifically with the Cornbury bribe.

On the morning of May 7, 1707, representatives of the assembly and Cornbury met face to face. Speaker Samuel Jenings, a leader of the West Jersey Quakers, bearded the Governor. An account of the day says Jenings was "undaunted" by the angry interruptions and a "countenance of sternness and authority." When he finished denouncing the Governor to his face, Cornbury is said to have remarked that "Jenings had impudence enough to face the Devil."

Five days later, Cornbury again faced the assembly and gave his answer. "You have squandered away your time in hawking after Imaginary Grievances," he told them. He urged that Quakers be refused seats in the assembly for violations of the Militia Act. And he read to Jenings, Lewis Morris and others the Queen's instructions for the government of the colony.

Mention of the Queen did not daunt the bold New

It was said that when Cornbury dressed as a woman, he fancied he resembled the Queen

Jerseyans. Lewis Morris was delegated to answer, and he spoke with a bluntness that made the Governor's faction gasp. He "told his Lordship that the Queen's orders and instructions did not concern or affect them, nor should it . . . any further than were warranted by law." That last phrase may have softened the statement enough to save Morris had he ever been charged with treason, but he had in effect defied the Queen herself—an act that horrified conservative royalists in his audience.

With the Governor and the assembly deadlocked and hating each other, the assembly now decided to lay the colony's grievances before the Secretary of State in England and, through him, before the Crown. Lewis Morris drew up a long and detailed complaint. He recited the story of the "blind tax," listed all Cornbury's misdeeds, and said the Quakers especially were "unwilling to raise a support [pay the salary] for a wretch who by the whole conduct of his life had evinc't y^t he had no regard to honor or virtue."

On this foundation, Morris plunged ahead to reveal a scandal that had been the talk of both New York and New Jersey. He told the Secretary of State of Cornbury's "dressing publickly in women's clothes every day and putting a stop to all Publique business while he is pleasing himself with y^t peculiar but detestable magot."

Cornbury had indeed been noted for this peculiar trait. It was said that, when he dressed himself up like a woman, he fancied that he resembled his cousin the Queen. In any event, he had been seen time and again parading in women's garb along the ramparts of his New York fort. When his wife had died in 1706, he had attended her funeral dressed as a woman.

Having exposed all, Lewis Morris concluded his long bill of complaint by demanding that Lord Cornbury be dismissed and a new governor appointed.

This dynamite-laden letter had its effect. Cornbury was removed as governor in 1708 and ordered back to England. And the hell-raising New Jerseyans long took pride in the fact that they had chased out of their colony even so prominent a person as the cousin of the Queen.

eight

How Life
Was Lived

What was life like in the Jerseys of this time, around the turn of the century?

It was still largely a frontier life, but gradually the land was filling up. A population study made in 1698 showed, surprisingly enough, that New Jersey was more thickly settled than New York. The two Jersey colonies, East and West, then had some twelve thousand families; New York had only five thousand.

Probably one reason for the faster settlement of New Jersey was its relative freedom from Indian wars. The Lenni-Lenapé, as has been said, were much less warlike than the Iroquois tribes of New York, and the early settlers of New Jersey always made it a policy to try to deal fairly with the Indians. The Quakers, Baptists and Puritans— the first settlers—did not seize the lands they wanted; they always bargained with the Indians and bought from them.

This did not mean that there was never trouble, that there were never misunderstandings. There were. Sometimes the Indian and the white man had different ideas about what had been included in a sale.

To the Indian, the sale of land meant just that—the sale of land. To the white man, it meant something else again. The white man, when he bought a tract of land, considered it and everything on it his—the wildlife, the fish in the streams, the fruit on the trees. But the Indian, having sold the land, often felt that he had a perfect right to hunt and fish on it. It was quite difficult at times to get him to understand that he was, in the white man's eyes, a trespasser and poacher.

An amusing difficulty of this kind took place on Sandy Hook, where a man named Hartshorne had bought a tract from the Indians. The Indians kept returning to hunt and fish on Hartshorne's land, and they liked especially to gather the wild beach plums that grew on low bushes sprouting from the sandy soil. Hartshorne protested these invasions of his property, and many discussions were held. The beach plums especially became a sore point. The Indians insisted they should have the right to gather them, and serious trouble seemed to be in the making. Finally, to avoid this, Hartshorne made a second purchase from the Indians. This time, he paid them thirteen shillings for the right to everything on his land, including the plums.

Payments to the Indians took various forms. Sometimes a tract large enough for the settlement of a town would be bought for a barrel of cider. At other times, ready-made coats, kettles, even jew's harps would be given in payment. Sometimes these deals had unfortunate side effects. In 1678 a conference was held in Burlington between the settlers and the Indians because the Indians had gotten smallpox from some ready-made coats the English had sold them. This was

a disease unknown to the Indians before the white man came, and it was especially deadly to them, often wiping out nearly a whole tribe.

In this conference, after much discussion, the Indians finally realized that the English had had no intention of infecting them. One chief rose and said:

"We are willing to have a broad path for you and us to walk in; and if an Indian is asleep in this path, the Englishman shall pass him by and do him no harm; and if an Englishman is asleep in the path, the Indian shall pass him by and say, 'He is an Englishman; he is asleep; let him alone; he loves to sleep!' It shall be a plain path. There must not be in this path a stump to hurt our feet."

The conference ended with the two parties exchanging presents and parting as friends. The idea for "a broad path for you and us to walk in"—the idea that there was a lot of land and room enough for all—was the basis for the continuing friendly relationship between the settlers and the Indians in New Jersey.

After the first settlers bought their town sites from the Indians, the land was divided. The practice varied somewhat from town to town, but in general the procedure was this:

A rough survey of the land was made, and the area was divided into three general categories. First, there were what were called the "town lots," the site of the future village. On these, the settler would build his home and a cowshed, and raise food in his garden. Next, there was meadow or marsh land where cattle could be pastured. And, third, there were "upland" lots for the planting of wheat, rye and corn.

When the land had been surveyed and divided, a draw-

The Lenni Lenape believed they had the right to hunt and fish on land even after they had sold it

ing of lots was held. The "town lots" were numbered, and numbered slips of paper would be put into a bag from which the settlers would draw them out one by one. The same procedure would then be followed for the division of the meadow and "upland" acreage.

These lots were all of good size. The "town lots" were smallest, but they were seldom less than six acres and sometimes more than that. In Woodbridge, for example, the "town lots" varied in size from 10 to 17 acres, and the first settlers were granted in addition 40 acres of meadowland and 240 "upland" acres.

The difference in the size of the holdings was explained by differences in the quality of the land. In settling Woodbridge, the settlers met in town meeting and ordered that if one lot was considered more fertile than another, the surveyors were "to add so much in quantity to the bad lot that it may countervail the goodness of the other." It sometimes happened, after a town was settled, that the residents found they lacked artisans with special skills. Perhaps they needed a blacksmith or a mason or a shipwright. Sometimes, to encourage such skilled workers to come to the town and settle, the citizens in town meeting would vote to make them a present of several acres of land.

After the first settlements, East and West Jersey developed in different ways. In West Jersey, for the most part large estates became larger. In East Jersey, they were gradually split up into smaller and smaller holdings. Religion had much to do with this. The Quakers forbid one of their faith to marry a Presbyterian or a Baptist or an Episcopalian. Quakers must marry Quakers. And so it came about that when a daughter married, her husband was often a young man from another landowning Quaker family. In this way estates were joined into ever larger estates, and an aristocratic, plantation-owning class developed.

East Jersey, which from the start was the more thickly

populated part of the state, followed a different pattern. Here, when the first settlers purchased land from the Indians, they bought huge tracts, much larger than they could use at the time. The leftover land was called "common land," owned by the village, and this, too, could be sectioned off and disposed of as the town grew.

These newly divided "upland" acres were, of course, farther and farther away from the original village. And so it happened that a settler in Woodbridge, for instance, might find himself possessed of fields near what is now Rahway, five miles away. Traveling five miles out and back on foot or horseback took several working hours out of the day, and so either one of two things happened. Perhaps the settler had a son who wanted to get married. Those distant "upland" acres were something of a nuisance—and so the father might give them to the son to get started in life. Or, as sometimes happened, the original settler might decide that it would be simpler to dispose of his "town lot" property and move out to his field acres, building there. Thus, by the mid-1680s, a new term came into being—the word "farm." The towns remained, but they became less and less the collection of "home lots" that they had been originally, and they became more and more what they have remained ever since—the centers of business and trade.

As land ownership changed, so did the homes of the settlers. The first settlers had had to be content with the fast construction of wigwam-type houses, made by tying the tops of young saplings together and filling in the walls with sod. Such homes could sometimes be built in a single day. But they were damp, cold, drafty and highly uncomfortable. As soon as possible, the settlers built better homes.

The typical, "better" home of the period was the so-called palisade home. Trunks of trees would be split and driven into the ground as close together as possible. The outer walls so formed would be bolted to an inner frame

made of similar split and axe-hewn tree trunks. The chinks between the split trees that formed the outer walls would be filled with clay or sod to keep out the wind and rain. Wood would be spilt into shingles to make a roof. A typical palisade house in 1685 was described as "twenty-four foot long and fifteen foot wide, containing a hall and kitchen, both in one, and a chamber and a study. . . ."

Later, in the early 1700s, clapboard and shingled houses were built. The clapboards were often crudely hewn with an axe out of tree trunks. One edge of each plank was thinner than the other so that the boards, when placed as siding on a house, would overlap, the thicker part of one plank

Like other settlements in New Jersey, Woodbridge became a center of business and trade

coming down over the thinner side of its neighbor. This, in theory, made a tight house. But the trouble was that many of the planks, hewn from trees just as they stood, had crooks in them. Much green lumber was used, and this warped and shrank as it seasoned. So gaps developed between the clapboards. Though these were filled in with a mixture of clay, straw and lime, there were almost always chinks through which the winter winds whistled, carrying dustings of snow.

These "better" homes still remained generally poor homes. They had few comforts. Glass had to be imported from England since it was not made in the colony. It was rare and extremely costly, and only the well-to-do could afford it. And so, in most homes, windows were small and few, and they were covered with oiled paper. Screens were unknown, and in the hot Jersey summers flies and mosquitoes in black swarms invaded the homes and threatened to bite the settlers to death. In the entire state, few homes could boast carpets on the floor. Fewer still had wallpaper or curtains. It is doubtful if, in the whole state, one could have found a single bathtub.

A settler might own broad acres, a sizable house—and still be almost poor as far as the possession of worldly goods went. When the early settlers died, inventories of estates showed how little they actually owned. John Fenwick, the founder of Salem, for example, left personal possessions that were valued at only about twenty English pounds.

Another typical example was the estate of Peter Gordon, who died in 1725. A Scotch settler, Gordon was known in

The Wick house (above), a typical farmhouse of the time, was built in 1750

The living-and-dining room of the Wick house (left)

Upper Freehold Township as "a planter," a term that would indicate he was a big man in the area. When he died, he left broad acres and an eight-room house, but that was about all except for a bed and bed hangings, a small old bed, a chest, two boxes, a small table, four new chairs, four old chairs, a loom, a wheel for spinning, and a wool-reel.

The house that Gordon left remained in the family until 1753, when it was sold to Robert Imlay. He died a year later, and the inventory of his estate showed only these items and the price placed upon them: "two feather beds and bedding, 14 pounds; one case of drawers and chest and table, 3 pounds." And then there was this significant entry: "One Negro wench and child, 40 pounds."

Though it has been generally forgotten today, New Jersey throughout all the early years of its history was a slaveowning state. Slavery was encouraged from the start as a way to speed up the conquest and development of the wild land. When Berkeley and Carteret first acquired the colony, they offered each new settler, not just 150 acres of land for himself, but an additional 150 acres for every full-grown male slave he brought with him and 75 acres for each child slave. When Queen Anne named Lord Cornbury governor, she stressed that he was to encourage the slave trade as a way to obtain the laborers needed in the new land.

With such royal backing there grew up a direct slave trade with Africa. A structure that was then called "a bar-

Built in 1685, this house, elaborate for its day, was the home of a wealthy distiller. Later, it was owned by Thomas Revel, the registrar of the West Jersey proprietors

racks" was built at Perth Amboy to house the African Negroes until they could be sold and dispersed on the farms. Even the Quakers at first saw nothing wrong with owning slaves. But in the early 1700s their consciences began to prick them. Slavery was denounced at their yearly meetings, and finally, about 1750, they decreed that no person owning slaves could continue in good standing in the church. The Quakers, however, were in advance of their time. In the colony as a whole most persons saw nothing wrong with owning Negro slaves—or Indians or redemptioners either, for that matter.

Not very much is known about the Indian slaves beyond the fact that they existed. They were probably few in number. Since the Jersey colonists and the Indians lived peaceably together, it is clear that the settlers did not go out to attack and enslave the Indians as the Spaniards had done in the Caribbean. What seems to have happened is that the Lenni-Lenapé, in occasional wars with other tribes, sometimes took prisoners and made a profit out of them by selling them to the white settlers. The traffic grew to the point that, when the assembly met in Burlington in 1704, it considered a bill to regulate the treatment of slaves—and it included Indians as well as Negroes.

The redemptioners were more numerous by far than the Indian slaves. A redemptioner was simply a poor person who had had no money with which to pay for his passage to America. He signed an agreement with a ship captain in England, giving the captain the right to "sell" him in America to get the passage money. The captains, of course, always wanted to sell the redemptioners for as much money as they could, and so the redemptioners would have to work for years for their masters until the debt was paid off.

The lot of the redemptioner was sometimes worse than that of the Negro slave for one very simple reason. The landowner owned the slave for the rest of the slave's life, but he only owned the redemptioner for a limited period of years. He had to get the most work out of him in that time. When owners were cruel or greedy, the system resulted in redemptioners being almost worked to death. Still, so great was the lure of freedom and opportunity in a new world that all kinds of persons took this desperate means of getting here—mechanics, laborers, professional men, even school teachers.

The treatment of redemptioners became so bad that laws were finally passed to protect them. One provided that no redemptioner who was seventeen or older at the time he was sold could be worked as a slave for more than four years. Another required his master, when his time expired, to give him "two good suits of clothing, suitable for a servant, one good ax, one good hoe, and seven bushels of Indian corn." With this start in life, many a redemptioner went out, found himself a piece of land and established his own home and family. Sometimes such a redemptioner prospered so well that he married a daughter of his former master and became a big man in the community.

Life as it was lived in those days was, of necessity, close to the land. The typical settler grew practically all his own food. Beans, potatoes, turnips, carrots and cabbage raised in the garden were regular parts of the diet. There was usually fresh deer or bear meat gotten from hunting in the forests. Fish and meats, particularly pork, were salted to preserve them. There was usually plenty of rye bread and milk. Butter was a rarity. Fruits like apples and peaches were sometimes preserved in stone jugs, but usually, like most of the home-grown vegetables, they were eaten only in season.

There was in those days no means of refrigeration. It was not until shortly before the Revolution that the first mention was made of an "ice house"—a structure sheltering a straw-lined pit in the ground, where ice, cut from the ponds and lakes, could be stored so that it would not melt and could be taken out for use during the warmer months.

In such a life, each family supplied most of its own needs. The women spun their own thread on looms, and from this they wove cloth. This "homespun" and the skins and furs of animals provided most of the clothing. Occasionally, shoes might be bought from a local shoemaker; nails and horseshoes from a local blacksmith; wheels for a wagon or cart from the local wheelwright. But when such extra items had to be purchased, they were paid for, not in cash which few persons had, but in meat or garden produce.

In Woodbridge, for example, when it became necessary to buy a quantity of ammunition, the town meeting instructed the constable to pay for it "in wheat and pork out of the Treasury." The minister's salary was "in the current pay of the country," a term that meant pork, beans, peas, wheat and other provisions.

Much of the community life centered around the church. In all parts of the colony, whatever the faith, religious influence was strong. It showed in many ways, most strikingly, perhaps, in the practice of giving children Biblical names or names meant to express a religious faith. Living in the Lippincott family in Shrewsbury in 1683 were Freedom, Remembrance and Restore. Jedediah Allen, of neighboring Navesink, had children named Experience, Ephraim, Judah and Patience. There were Exercise and Elisone Cole, daughters of Jacob. And among the children of Thomas Thomson, of Elizabeth, in 1675 were Aaron, Moses and Hur.

Religious feeling ran at a hot pitch in the strict Puritan settlements of East Jersey. The Puritans who had settled Newark had been determined to keep their harsh faith unchanged. But they could not keep Newark forever to themselves. People of other faiths, including some Hugenots from France, came in and settled. In time the church and town, which originally had been one unit, with the church running everything, became separate and distinct bodies as the Puritans' grip on the life of the community weakened.

The bitterness of the break with the sternness of the old order rose to a peak in the case of Colonel Josiah Ogden. The colonel was a pillar of the church, a man of wealth, a leader in the community. He had represented Newark in the assembly from 1716 to 1721. He was the last man one might have expected to break the Puritans' sacred rule of rules—that no work should be performed on Sunday.

But the late summer and fall of 1733 was a bad one and a testing time for rules. There had been days on end of steady rain. Colonel Ogden's wheat was in danger of rotting in the fields if he could not get it harvested. Then came a beautiful weekend, hot, sunny and dry. And the colonel, Lord's Day or no Lord's Day, went out and harvested his wheat.

His act soon had the whole community in an uproar. Followers of the pure faith were horrified, and they had Ogden brought up on charges before the congregation. A few decades earlier even so prominent a man as Colonel Ogden would doubtless have landed in the stocks for his offense. To the fanatics it seemed a sign of the looseness of the times that the congregation let the colonel off with nothing worse than a severe censure.

This, however, was not the end of it. The colonel considered he had only used sound common sense in harvesting his wheat on Sunday, when the weather had made it impossible for him to gather it at any other time. He and his supporters took a walk right out of the church. Soon the whole community was split into bitter, wrangling, pro-Ogden and anti-Ogden factions. The presbytery of the church tried to smooth things over by reversing the congregation and wiping out the motion of censure. But it was now too late.

A group of Anglicans, most of them well-to-do people, had

Ogden horrified the Puritans because he dared to harvest his wheat on a Sunday

settled along the Passaic River. Colonel Ogden and his supporters now joined forces with them and established an Episcopal church. Within a few years, they raised funds and built Trinity Church in Newark. This was an offense that, if anything, only increased the Puritans' outrage. The dispute continued for decades, down to the time of the Revolution. Friends, neighbors, relatives were split into warring factions. All because Colonel Ogden had harvested his wheat on a Sunday.

Such, then, was the life that was lived in East and West Jersey in the late 1600s and the early part of the following century.

If it had been possible to make a pictorial map of New Jersey at the time, this is what it would have shown:

Settlements were clustered for the most part along the deeper bays and rivers. Burlington, Salem and Perth Amboy were the largest towns. Perth Amboy was the principal port of East Jersey, and the town where the legislature and Supreme Court met. Burlington filled a simlar role in West Jersey. Salem was a major port and trading center.

There were other and smaller settlements: those along the Passaic around Newark and spreading out to Westfield and the Oranges; those that fanned out from the Woodbridge settlement; the Shrewsbury and Middletown villages in northern Monmouth County.

Most of the rest of the state was still a wilderness. Inland, in the heart of the state, there stretched a great, unsettled span of pine forest. The coast was a wild ribbon of sand dunes, long finger-shaped islands, marshes, rivers and bays.

From Sandy Hook to Cape May only a few beachmen, Indians and hunters roamed the sands. Shoals that stretched far out to sea along the Ocean and Atlantic County coasts made the Barnegat area the graveyard of shipping. Each winter brought its storms and wrecks, and mariners came to dread the term "Barnegat shoals" as they feared the devil.

For the better part of a century—indeed, almost to the mid-nineteenth century—this picturesque coastal area remained almost a barren waste. No crops could be grown in the sandy soil of the offshore barrier islands that separated the long bays of the mainland from the raging waves of the Atlantic. The high dunes were covered with a coarse grass, some hardy oaks and cedars. The oaks, much prized for the toughness of their wood, were cut for shipbuilding; the cedars made beautiful chests. But the only use that could be made of the tough dune grass was for the grazing of cattle, and so early settlers rowed cattle across to the outer islands in flat-bottomed scows. There, turned loose, they grew in time into herds of "wild cattle."

Though the area was a waste to the farmer, to the hunter it was a paradise. The "wild cattle" furnished him with food. Wild fowl were so plentiful they could sometimes be

Trinity Church was destroyed by fire in 1804. The tower is now part of the present church building

knocked on the head with a stick. The waters of the bays were filled with what one settler called "prodigious shoals" of fish. Oysters, clams, all kinds of shellfish were to be had for the gathering.

Whales were so numerous that they ranged all along the coast, poked their noses into New York Bay, entered Delaware Bay and even went far up the Delaware River. From the earliest days, settlers put out to sea in their small but strong boats to harpoon whales, for fortunes could be made from whalebone and whale oil. In 1693, the West Jersey legislature passed an act providing that any whalers not living in New Jersey or Pennsylvania who should "bring to shore any whale or whales in Delaware Bay . . . shall pay one full and entire tenth of all the oyl and bone made out of the said whale or whales unto the present Governor of this Province for the time being."

In a land so rich with natural bounties, it is little wonder that one of the early governors should write to the proprietors back in London in 1685: "There is not a poor body in all the province, nor [one] that wants." More than half a century later, another governor was to write that New Jerseyans were "the most Easie and happy people of any collony in North America."

nine

The
Colonial Wars

Those were wild and lawless days. In the late 1690s and early 1700s, pirates infested the New Jersey coast. And, in Europe, England was almost constantly at war, usually with France, sometimes with Spain. The result was that enemy privateers, barely one grade better than pirates, swarmed from Sandy Hook to Cape May.

The privateer was a privately owned war vessel. Such private warships were licensed by their own governments to capture ships and property of the enemy—but only of the enemy. They were not supposed to attack vessels of other nations. But many a privateersman, finding a fat and helpless merchantman rolling along in front of him, forgot this rule in his eagerness for plunder and became a pirate.

The rewards of such high seas action were tempting and tremendous. They were so tempting, in fact, that many a corrupt official during the colonial period actually had secret, hidden interests in pirate affairs—and so was more concerned with protecting the pirates than with catching them. The result was that throughout the 1690s and early 1700s, pirate vessels prowled constantly in Delaware Bay and the outer waters of New York harbor.

In 1699 Robert Quarry, vice-admiral of Pennsylvania, described how he had caught "4 more of the Pyrates at Cape May." He added: "I might have with Ease secured all the rest of them, and the Ship too," except for local officials. These officials, he wrote, had "Entertain'd the Pyrates, conveyed them from place to place, Furnish'd them with Provisions and Liquors, given them Intelligence and sheltered them from Justice. All the persons that I have employed in searching for and apprehending these Pyrates are abused and affronted and called Enemies to the Country for Disturbing and hindring honest men (as They are pleased to call the Pyrates)."

The pirates who preyed along the New Jersey coast at the time were sometimes welcomed in public by the governor of New York, always provided, of course, that they had paid their protection money. Ordinary "protections" were "commonly sold at one hundred dollars a man. For captains and others of high rank, the price was increased, usually involving open bribes of expensive gifts to the Governor and his family." One of the most notorious pirates of the day, Captain Tew, "was one of the Governor's favorite dinner guests and appeared publicly in his coach."

When England went to war with European powers, a plague of privateers was added to the plague of pirates. From 1702–1713, England and France waged what became known as Queen Anne's War, or the War of the Spanish Succession. Battle had hardly been joined before French privateers appeared off the New Jersey coast. In June, 1702, one bold French raider hove to off Sandy Hook and sent a raiding party ashore in boats. The privateersmen plundered two homes at "Neversinks," as the Navesink highlands then were called. Monmouth County militia gathered in force, and the invaders retreated to their boats. The privateer then sailed away.

The following month a French privateer from Bordeaux appeared off the Delaware capes, where she captured a merchant sloop. The privateer then cruised up the coast, chasing one vessel around Sandy Hook and into New York harbor and making several other captures. Three privateers were fitted out in New York to go after the raider, but before they could get to sea, the Frenchman had vanished.

This was a pattern that was to be repeated again and again along the wild New Jersey coast. The records of the time contain no mention of any other raids ashore like the

The notorious pirate Captain Tew was one of the governor's favorite dinner guests

one at Navesink, but in 1705 French privateers again had a field day, plundering shipping off the coast and then flitting off to their dens in the West Indies before ships could be armed to attack them.

One effect of such raids was to make the colonists eager to deliver a knockout blow against French-held Canada, the source of so much trouble. In 1709, when British authorities planned a big invasion of Canada, the New Jersey legislature voted to raise 3,000 pounds sterling to equip a force of 200 men. But after the money had been raised and the men enlisted, the British fleet was sent elsewhere—and, without the fleet, nothing could be attempted. The whole venture collapsed, much to the disgust of the colonists.

The fall of 1739 found England at war with Spain. Treaties between the two countries had stated that English vessels were not to trade with the Spanish-held islands in the West Indies. This rule had been ignored by smugglers from many of the American colonies, including New Jersey. Goods were constantly being smuggled into and out of the Spanish possessions. When Spain tried to search the smuggling vessels and seize their cargoes, war broke out.

Now Spanish privateers descended upon the New Jersey coast, just as the French had done earlier. In May, 1740, "three Sloops, a Snow and a Scooner" ranged along the coast, making several captures. Their successes were such that the New Jersey legislature voted 400 pounds to help equip two privateers "to look after these Spaniards." As usual, by the time the privateers were ready for sea, "these Spaniards" were long gone.

The British Admiralty now decided to send a fleet of thirty warships, loaded with several thousand troops, to attack Spanish strongholds in the West Indies. New Jersey joined eagerly in the enterprise. Three companies of New Jersey volunteers sailed down the Delaware late in 1740 and

War broke out when Spain tried to search the smuggling vessels

joined forces with another force of militia sailing from Perth
Amboy. The combined group joined up with the fleet of
Admiral Vernon at Jamaica on January 9, 1741, and sailed
with him for an attack on the Spanish stronghold of Cartagena.

Almost at once yellow fever broke out and swept through
the fleet. One thousand men died in ten days. Captains
Farmer and Thomas, of New Jersey, tried to inspire and
encourage their men, but the fever raged on, and the ranks
thinned as one man after another died. In the entire British
force, more than eight thousand died. The expedition had
to be abandoned, defeated by disease before it had ever felt

Spanish bullets. And of the New Jersey volunteers who had set out so bravely, few indeed were those who returned to their homes and fields.

In 1744 England again went to war with France in a conflict that became known as King George's War. This time, at the outset, with the horrors of the Cartagena expedition still fresh in mind, New Jersey was not willing to shoulder any of the burdens of war. Governor Lewis Morris, described by one writer as "little better than a common scold," was at odds with the assembly, in which ten of the twenty-two members were Quakers. These Quakers got enough other delegates to support them. When Governor Morris asked them to pass a bill to raise militia, they refused. The governor, in anger, then dismissed the assembly and sent it packing.

The result was that New Jersey had little to do with the first great victory of the war. In the spring of 1745, with Massachusetts leading the way, the American colonies planned an attack on the great French stronghold of Louisburg on Cape Breton Island off Nova Scotia, at the mouth of the St. Lawrence. New Jersey contributed 2,000 pounds, mostly in provisions and produce, to aid the endeavor, and a few New Jerseyans went along as volunteers. The colony as a whole, however, played only a minor role in the campaign that brought the fall of Louisburg on June 19, 1745.

The loss of this fortress roused the French to greater effort. A French war fleet was sent to the American coast, and French privateers again raided the shipping lanes around Sandy Hook and the capes of the Delaware. Faced with this kind of stepped-up menace, even the unwilling assembly gave in and voted to raise and equip a small army of militia.

The British generals were again dreaming their favorite dream of a major invasion of Canada. And New Jersey agreed to help. In June, 1746, the assembly issued a call for 500 militiamen. The great victory at Louisburg, however, had so excited the people that 650 men enlisted in five companies. They were provisioned with "192 barrels of powder, 110 barrels of beef, 60,000 pounds of biscuit, 2,000 gallons of rum and 3,000 pounds of tobacco. . . ." They were commanded by Colonel Peter Schuyler, who lived at Petersboro, near what is now Belleville. Early in September, "in their Complement of Battoes," they rowed away from Perth Amboy and headed up the Hudson to war.

The New Jersey troops joined New York forces at Albany. Here again, as happened so often in colonial history, they suffered the disappointment caused by poor planning on the highest British command level. The regular British troops, necessary for the planned attack on Canada, never did show up. The New Jersey militiamen had to spend a frigid winter guarding the New York frontier against French and Indian attacks. The supplies that they had been given at the start had not been meant to last for such a long time. Food ran out, their clothes were in tatters. They were cold, hungry— and unpaid.

Colonel Schuyler sent a petition to the governor and the legislature, describing the hardships of his men and pleading for supplies and money. But the assembly, which had already spent a large sum on a wasted enterprise, refused to act. Thus almost abandoned by their own legislators, the New Jersey troops threatened to mutiny in May, 1747. At this crisis, Colonel Schuyler dug down into his own pockets to put up the money to pay his men and supply their needs.

His example forced the hand of some of the other colonies that had been dealing in like hardhearted fashion with their soldiers. Governor Clinton, of New York, had pleaded with Colonel Schuyler not to pay his men, fearing two things. First, that once they were paid, they would pack up and go home. Secondly, that, if the Jersey troops were paid, other colonial militia in the same situation would demand their wages. The second of these fears turned out to be true. The New York troops did indeed raise a fuss, and Clinton had to find the money to pay them. But the Governor's first dread was never realized. The New Jerseyans did not go home. They stuck it out on the frontier around Saratoga until peace was signed in 1748.

The peace did not last long. By 1754 England and France were at war again in the long struggle that was to become known as the French and Indian War. It was the conflict that was finally to drive the French out of Canada, but before it was finished, the French had stirred up the Indians to set the frontiers aflame. Northern and western New Jersey were, in those days, a part of those frontiers.

When one thinks today of frontiersmen, one thinks of Daniel Boone and the Indian wars in Kentucky. It is hard to realize that, in the French and Indian War, the western frontier was just beyond the Delaware. Easton, Pennsylva-

Colonel Schuyler paid the soldiers out of his own pocket when the legislature refused to do so

nia, just across the river from Phillipsburg, was a true frontier town, squatting at the edge of the wilderness, with
Indians prowling only a few miles to the west. It was in
Easton that some of the finest long rifles were made. It was
from the high hills of Morris and Sussex counties in north-
western New Jersey that some of the finest scouts and woods-
men came.

The defeat of the British General Braddock, ambushed
in the Pennsylvania wilderness at the outset of the war, and
the threat that a wave of raiding Indians would soon be
thrown against settlements all along the frontier spurred
the New Jersey colonists to action.

In April, 1755, the legislature agreed to raise a force of
five hundred men under Colonel Schuyler to take part in
a planned attack on the great French fortress of Ticonderoga, commanding the Lake Champlain–Lake George invasion route into the heart of New York state. Such was the
alarm and excitement in New Jersey that a letter written
from Trenton in April reported "every body is willing to
contribute a Mite against the French and the Country
Fellows list like mad." The "Country Fellows," indeed,
could hardly wait to get into action, and by mid-May the
rolls of four of the five companies were nearly filled. And
late June saw Colonel Schuyler and his troops setting out
for Albany and the Ticonderoga campaign.

They had hardly left when Indian war parties descended
on the nearby Pennsylvania frontier, raiding, scalping and
burning just beyond the Delaware. By August, "on account
of the Scalping Indians," refugees were streaming in from
the back country and seeking safety across the river in New
Jersey. With their cattle, corn and whatever they could save
of their household goods, the survivors left "villages laid in
ashes," with "men, women and children cruelly mangled
and massacred . . . hacked, and covered all over with
wounds."

Darley—

The hit-and-run border raids continued into the fall. In early November, with rumors that new Indian war parties were on the way, Colonel John Anderson raised four hundred Sussex County militiamen and joined forces with one hundred and fifty Pennsylvanians to protect the frontier. The militiamen were short of powder. Hearing that some

The hit-and-run border raids continued

was stored with the Moravian missionaries at Bethlehem, Pennsylvania, Colonel Anderson sent an agent to try to purchase it. The Moravians refused to sell. No man to be trifled with in a crisis, Colonel Anderson then threatened to burn down their town about their ears unless they turned over the powder. And so, in the end, they did.

Anderson's force never did make contact with the Indians. After a useless search of the wilderness trails, Anderson decided that the rumors of a new attack must be false. Many of the militiamen were disbanded and sent to their homes. Then the Indians struck again. They burned the Moravian town of Gnadenhutten in Pennsylvania, only about thirty miles from Easton, and massacred all the inhabitants. Again the militia of Morris and Sussex counties were called back to duty. Again they swept the nearby Pennsylvania forests. Again the raiding Indians had vanished. But new refugees from the flaming Pennsylvania frontier fled into New Jersey. A series of crude frontier blockhouses was built at Broadheads, Calverts Mills and other places to protect the now almost completely exposed settlements of Sussex County.

While trying to defend her own territory, New Jersey was engaged up to the hilt in efforts to win the larger war. Colonel Schuyler's men had been part of the army that forced the French to give up Fort Ticonderoga after a few skirmishes in the summer campaign of 1755. But the French and their Indian allies still menaced the frontier settlements of central New York. And so in April, 1756, the New Jersey legislature sent another armed force under Colonel Schuyler to Albany to help fight the northern war on which the security of New Jersey's own frontiers so greatly depended.

These efforts required the spending of a great sum of money. The legislature passed a bill to raise 17,500 pounds to support the 750 men in service for the 1756 campaign. This was added to 57,500 pounds voted earlier, and before the war was over, New Jersey's contribution was to be one of the heaviest of all the American colonies. It was estimated that the New Jersey war effort cost five dollars a head for every man, woman and child—and this in a colony in which money was scarce, in a colony that had always objected heavily to taxation of any kind.

But the need was great, the hour perilous. The success of the northern Indians in raiding the Pennsylvania frontier had stirred up the usually peaceful Lenni-Lenapé. Many of them now joined the raiding parties, and in May, 1756, Indian warriors struck at Paulins Kill in Sussex County. Fortunately, the residents had enough warning so that some sixty families living in the area could flee to safety in Amwell, but the homes they left behind were burned, their fields laid waste.

New Jersey was furious. For the first time, the legislature denounced the Lenni-Lenapé for having violated their treaties and called them "Enemies, Rebels, and Traitors to his most sacred Majesty." A reward of 150 Spanish dollars was offered to anyone, except a soldier in service, who took prisoner a male Indian above fifteen years of age. A reward of 130 Spanish dollars was offered for killing such an Indian, and a like reward of 130 Spanish dollars was to be paid for the body of any Indian, male or female, under the age of fifteen.

The major action of the 1756 campaign was, however, on the New York frontier, and it was a disaster. Colonel Schuyler's New Jersey troops had been made part of the garrison of a fort at Oswego. There they sat under bungling British generalship, doing almost nothing and waiting to be gobbled up. The French were eager for the meal. In August an army of three thousand French and Indians struck at the open fort. Its outer works fell within twenty-four hours. On August 14, the entire garrison of one thousand four hundred men surrendered. The New Jersey troops captured at Oswego were imprisoned in Quebec, where Colonel Schuyler spent his own money, as he had done previously at Albany, to see that his men were kept in food and clothing.

The following year brought further disaster. The French swept down the Lake Champlain invasion route and attacked Fort Ticonderoga. New Jersey troops were there—

three hundred and fifty of them under the command of Colonel John Parker—and by the time Ticonderoga fell, all but seventy-five of them had been killed. The French and Indians swept on to the southern end of Lake George. Southern New York and New Jersey began to tremble at the thought of a full-scale invasion.

New Jersey prepared for an even greater effort. One thousand men were called to arms for the campaign of 1758. The colony promised to provide one coat, a pair of cloth breeches, a pair of buckskin breeches, a white and a checked shirt, two pairs of shoes, two pairs of stockings, a hat, blanket, canteen and hatchet for each recruit. A bounty of twelve pounds and "a dollar to drink His Majesty's Health" was offered to all who promised to serve until September 15.

Late in May, the New Jersey Provincial Regiment set out for Albany, clad in "Uniform blue, faced with red, grey Stockings and Buckskin Breeches. . . . They are accounted a Parcel of robust sturdy Men." This was the first mention of a uniform that was to become famous in the Revolution —the "Jersey Blues."

The campaign of 1758, however, brought more defeat and heartbreak. The British tried to retake Ticonderoga, but their generalship was bad and the French, with much smaller forces, threw them back. This time, fortunately, New Jersey losses were light, for "the Jersey Blues" had been held in reserve and had not been in the heaviest fighting. At home, the Sussex frontier still suffered from hit-and-run Indian attacks, but the local militia fought back courageously and the Indians had some losses.

This brave resistance, plus some skillful handling of the Indian problem by New Jersey authorities, finally succeeded in cooling off the Indian war. In October and early November, 1758, Governor Bernard of New Jersey and other officials met with two hundred Indian chiefs, representing thirteen nations, at "the forks of the Delaware" near Easton.

The chiefs of the more warlike New York tribes spoke for the New Jersey Delawares, who, as "old women," were supposed to need stronger hands to settle their affairs. Governor Bernard told the chiefs that New Jersey would spend 1,600 pounds to buy from them all the rest of the land they claimed in the colony and to settle any wrongs they might feel they had.

The Indians seemed to be impressed, for after much poker-faced consideration, one of the chiefs of the Six Nations rose and said:

"Brethren, we now remove the hatchet out of your heads, that was struck into it by our cousins, the Delawares. It was a French hatchet they unfortunately made use of. . . . We take it out of your heads and bury it underground. Our cousins the Delawares have assured us they will never think of war against their brethren the English any more, but will employ their thoughts about peace and cultivating friendship with them. . . ."

Governor Bernard asked that the Delawares be required to return any prisoners that they still held. One of the great chiefs, appearing surprised at this, scolded the Delawares for not having already released the prisoners as, it seems, they had promised to do. With the Delawares soundly told off and promising to release their captives, the meeting ended in friendly fashion—and, with it, the last Indian war in New Jersey.

The other and greater struggle—the battle between England and France for the possession of North America—was to continue for five more long and bloody years. In this war, New Jersey continued to do her part.

In 1759, though the colony had already lost one thousand men out of fifteen thousand of all ages available for military duty, a call was issued for another one thousand militia. Barracks were built at Burlington, Trenton, New Brunswick, Perth Amboy and Elizabeth. Colonel Peter Schuyler, freed from imprisonment and a great hero in both New York and New Jersey, once more took command. Colonel Schuyler and his New Jersey troops formed a part of the British and colonial army that invaded Canada and brought about the fall of Quebec, where the colonel had been so long held prisoner.

In 1762, Spain entered the war against England, and a regiment of "Jersey Blues" joined British forces in the West Indies. There they had a hand in the capture of Morro Castle, the fortress guarding Cuba's capital city of Havana. New Jersey losses in this campaign were light, for the Spaniards did not fight well. And the following year, the war ended.

It ended in triumph. It ended with England in control of both Canada and the American colonies. And it ended by giving birth to a host of new problems that were to lead, in time, to the Revolution.

ten

The
Second Revolution

To the war abroad was added rioting and confusion at home. The mid-1700s, so filled with desperate battle against the French and Indians, were also at times marked by a revolution on the home front—a kind of second revolution that was more widespread and more violent than that of the early 1700s.

The causes were much the same. They were rooted in the continuing quarrel over land ownership and in the old question of the right of the proprietors to require that everyone should pay a quit rent.

Following the recall of Lord Cornbury in 1708, royal governor followed royal governor. All ruled in a double way. They held two separate commissions. One made them governors of New York; the second, governors of New Jersey. The effect was to tie New Jersey to New York's apron strings. Though the Crown recognized New Jersey as a separate colony, the fact that the colony was ruled by New York's governor robbed it of its independence and made it a kind of second-class territory. In one of their petitions to the King, the people through their representatives in the assembly put it this way: "The heart burnings amongst the Inhabitants, and the Grievances of the Country are not known and understood, or at least never regarded, the governor being free from the Noise and Clamour of them, at New York."

This second-class status was enough to annoy the independent New Jerseyans. But it was the conduct of many of the royal governors that raised their temperatures to fever pitch. Too many governors, like Richard Ingoldsby who followed Lord Cornbury, seemed to look upon New Jersey only as a province in which to fatten their own pockets. Ingoldsby had a field day granting licenses for settlers to buy tracts from the Indians, in complete disregard of the proprietors' claim to the ownership of all the undeveloped land. And his appointments to high public office led to scandal. Some of his favorites held as many as nine— one even had eleven—public jobs. In all, there were just 90 persons holding 196 public offices.

This became too much, and Ingoldsby's brief reign was ended in 1710. Other governors succeeded him for short and generally unsatisfactory terms. New Jersey through its assembly continued to bombard the Crown with appeals that it be given truly separate standing as a colony, with its own governor. Finally, a petition sent to England in 1736 was listened to, and Lewis Morris—he who had written the bitter attack on Cornbury—was named in 1738 to be the first independent governor of New Jersey under the Crown.

Now there occurred one of the strangest turnabouts in New Jersey's colonial history. Lewis Morris had been generally known as a man of the people. As a boy, he had run away from home in New York and had lived for a time in Virginia, where he had come to hate the harshness of colonial rule. Though he had sometimes been part of officialdom, as in his role in the Middletown riots of 1700, he had time and again sided with the popular cause. In his opposition to Cornbury, he had become something of a popular hero. His appointment as governor was received, therefore, with much rejoicing. But hardly had he entered on his new duties, when he fell out with the assembly and began to act much like other royal governors.

Many have thought that possibly age had changed Lewis Morris. Whatever idealism and drive he had possessed in his younger days was gone. He was now governor. The title perhaps went to his head, and he wanted honors and money. Within a year, in the voice of "the common scold" that some

Lewis Morris sided with the proprietors during the bitter land disputes

called him, he was complaining "of the insincerity and ignorance of the people" and of the "inclination of the meanest" to have sole control of the affairs of government. And in the bitter land disputes of the time, he quickly sided with the proprietors, where the money was, rather than with the people, where at least some of the right was.

There were at this time five main political groupings in the colony. At the top were the proprietors, owners of all the undeveloped land, a wealthy class generally at odds with the rest of the people. Opposed to them were the old Elizabethtown-Nicolls faction, who fought for the rights of the small landowner. Sometimes linked with them was a group of small farmers around the Oranges. The fourth faction was composed mostly of lawless squatters who had gone into the wilderness and taken up land in Hunterdon, Morris and Sussex counties without paying any attention to the rights of the proprietors. In the middle ground, taking as little stand as possible on the claims of the warring groups, was a large number of peaceable, law-abiding Quakers.

The quarrels over land ownership and payment of quit rents had quieted down after "the revolution" of the early 1700s, but all the old issues remained alive under the surface, ready to explode in new trouble. And the steady growth of New Jersey soon made the explosion certain.

The proprietors' shortsighted policies were at the bottom of the difficulty. There was a lot of land in New Jersey—and yet, in another way, there was little. The proprietors had approved the sale of only 420,000 acres of land in the 7,836 square-mile colony. All the rest they still held in their tight, land-grabbing fists. As more colonists arrived, as the population grew, the need for more land became acute. This growing need boosted the price of land, which may have been fine for the proprietors, but certainly was not fine for settlers who wanted farms. These conditions were made to

order for the growth of rebels who would do almost anything they could to break the proprietors' hold on the land.

The first act of open rebellion came on July 1, 1734, when
the Elizabethtown Associates held a meeting to sell off land
they still claimed under the old Nicolls patent. The acres
they were selling were part of the proprietors' holdings in
Somerset County. There was not too much doubt in anyone's mind about this. The proprietors had taken several
cases to court after their original defeat in the early 1700s.
The courts were now upholding their claims. These favorable court decisions had led the proprietors, beginning
about 1725, to defend their land titles with vigor and to
bring ever more suits. All of this was well known—so much
so that one Elizabethtown salesman gave customers this
pitch: the timber on the land that was being sold was more
than worth the purchase price, and the proprietors could
be tied up in the courts so long that the timber could be
cut and sold, and the profit reaped, before they could get a
court order to stop the practice. This was one way, said
this sly salesman, to fight the proprietors "with their own
Estates."

As soon as the Elizabethtowners started to sell land in
Somerset, the proprietors counterattacked. They hired spies
to watch every move the Elizabethtowners made. As soon as
a surveyor was caught trespassing on land claimed by the
proprietors, a suit was brought, and action was started to
throw settlers off the disputed acres.

All of this was enough to make the pot boil and bubble,
but now the proprietors, in their stubbornness, added another explosive to the stew. They had not bothered to collect quit rents—that halfpenny an acre a man was supposed
to pay even after he had purchased his property—for a number of years. It took more time and trouble and expense
to collect the quit rents than they were worth, the proprietors had decided. But now someone added up the quit rents

that were due and figured that the proprietors had 10,000 pounds coming to them. This was a truly princely figure in those days, and the proprietors began to enjoy the prospect of such a windfall. So they started actions to collect. And when they did, everybody hated them. Not just the Elizabethtown group, not just the Hunterdon-Morris-Sussex group. But everybody.

It was not possible to avoid a showdown. The only question was how violent a showdown it would be. Perhaps a governor more in the middle than Lewis Morris might have cooled some of the passions. But Morris was far from in the middle. Even before he became governor, he had involved himself in the land situation on the side of the proprietors. In 1735 he had sent his son, Lewis, into the West Jersey Society's "great tract" of wilderness acres in Hunterdon County. The son had found that ninety-eight families were occupying 13,000 acres of land to which they had no shadow of title. In another part of the frontier country, he reported, the people had smeared their faces black and had driven off agents of the proprietors. They had even threatened one of the most powerful of the proprietors, Colonel Daniel Coxe, Jr., with assassination.

When he became governor, Lewis Morris promptly began to act in his official capacity, practically as a servant of the proprietors. He named his son chief justice to rule over the colony's court system. He packed the council, the upper chamber of the legislature, with hand-picked agents of the proprietors. He thus made certain that, between the council and his own powers as governor, any action that the people might take in the assembly would be blocked.

The proprietors now started a flock of lawsuits. With Lewis Morris, Jr., sitting as chief justice, they had little trouble getting favorable verdicts in the courts. And so, by 1745, they could boast that they had driven the Elizabethtown men back from holdings thirty miles outside the town to a line within three or four miles of town. What this meant, of course, was that the common people had no avenue through which to right what they felt were the wrongs against them. Action by the assembly was blocked; the courts were packed against them. Only violence was left. And it was not long in coming.

The first riot occurred in Newark on September 19, 1745. Samuel Baldwin had been arrested for cutting wood on the proprietors' land, and he had been thrown into the Newark jail pending trial. A small mob gathered, attacked and broke open the jail—and freed Baldwin.

Four months later, when officials identified three of the ringleaders and arrested them, a large crowd gathered "armed with Cudgels . . . and rescued the Prisoners in a very violent Manner." The sheriff hurried off to the jail and raised a force of thirty militiamen to guard it. The mob, flushed with its first success in rescuing the three prisoners, gathered about the jail and soon swelled in size to about three hundred persons.

In late afternoon, shouting and screaming, this angry mob flung itself against the defenders of the jail, and hand-to-hand fighting broke out. The thirty militiamen and the sheriff were quickly overcome, the jail cells broken open, and all the prisoners released. Then the mob marched away in triumph, having performed a deed that was to be the talk of the colony for weeks.

In March, 1746, the assembly met, and Governor Morris, in his opening speech, denounced the riots as "high treason." He warned that such occurrences were but "too likely to end in Rebellion and throwing off His Majesty's Authority."

The proprietors, panicky now, wanted harsh action taken to put down this new "revolution." They got a bill introduced in the assembly that was so severe it raised a howl of protest. It provided that if twelve or more persons met and refused to disperse, they should be judged criminals and be put to death without benefit of clergy.

At this point, with the storm breaking out on all sides, Governor Morris died. He was succeeded by Acting Governor John Hamilton. Hamilton, too, tried to get the assembly to pass strong antiriot legislation, but the assembly held off. In September Hamilton repeated his request—and the assembly, its refusal.

Now there was more violence. The Somerset County jail was broken into, the prisoners freed. Striking back, Governor Hamilton ordered the sheriffs to arrest all persons whom they thought to be assembling in a "Riotus Manner."

But matters were now out of hand. The revolt spread. In the spring of 1747, the Morris County squatters became so bold that they were not content with defending their own homes. They began to attack and drive out the proprietary land holders.

Despite this new trouble, the assembly again refused to act when it met in May, 1747. On June 17, Acting Governor Hamilton died, and his successor, John Reading, had hardly gotten into the governor's chair when the worst of the riots broke out in Perth Amboy.

This key East Jersey port was the stronghold of the proprietary party. Its officials had been most active in trying to arrest rioters. They had tracked down and arrested John Bainbridge, Jr., as one of the leaders in the Somerset riot, and they had thrown Bainbridge into jail to await trial. An account of the day tells what happened next.

A mob of about one hundred and fifty "Armed with Great Clubs came into town on horse back." The sheriff faced them and read the governor's proclamation ordering the arrest of all rioters. The account then quotes the unhappy sheriff about what happened next: "I was knocked down & have a Grievous Wound in my head, and they also Struck the Mayor, broke one of the Constable's head, beat several others and then violently with a Sledge and Iron Barr & a Hatchet broke open the Outward & Inner Doors of the Gaol, took out the prisoner and Carried him off Huzzaing."

The names of twenty of the rioters were obtained, and the judge ordered the grand jury to indict them for high treason. But the grand jury, composed largely of common people, sympathized with the rioters and refused to act.

Shortly afterward, there came a shift in official policy. The Crown named Jonathan Belcher as the new governor, and at the outset Belcher threw his weight behind the cause of the people. He made friends with members of the assembly, and it finally passed an antiriot bill. It was a mild measure, robbed of any real force by the assembly's failure to appropriate any money to enforce it. But, in return for this face-saving favor, Governor Belcher offered a full pardon to all who had taken part in the riots, provided they asked forgiveness.

These measures cooled off the passions that had nearly torn the colony apart. The proprietors dropped the attempt to collect quit rents, thus taking the sting out of their actions for many. They continued to press some of their suits over land titles, but their influence with the courts was now less. They sometimes won, and they sometimes lost, in a series of confused legal battles that lasted down to the time of the Revolution. What was important at the time was that the violence had ended.

The riots had again shown, however, the fierce independence of the New Jersey colonists and their willingness to riot and fight for what they regarded as their rights. There had been a sound prophecy, perhaps sounder than he knew, in Lewis Morris's statement that such actions were all "too likely to end in Rebellion and throwing off His Majesty's Authority."

eleven

The Final Rebellion

England's great triumph in the French and Indian War had left her with a mighty empire—and with all of a mighty empire's problems.

The costs of the war had been enormous. England had been bled white. She was so heavily in debt that, even with the coming of peace, taxes had to be raised—and the average Englishman howled. She had acquired so much new territory (the vast land of Canada, for example) that she had to keep large overseas garrisons. These cost tremendous amounts of money. It was only natural, then, from the viewpoint of the mother country, that the colonies in America should be taxed to bear at least a part of this burden.

But the colonies saw it differently. They had sacrificed thousands of lives in the common defense. They had taxed themselves heavily and gone into debt. They had seen their frontiers laid waste, and they had had to provide largely for their own defense. They felt that they had done their share. Besides, they were not anxious to have British garrisons quartered among them, a possible threat to the liberties of the people. And so they rebelled at the prospect of new and heavy tax burdens.

Though New Jersey was not a leader in the new protests, a large part of her people felt much as those in the other colonies did. New Jersey had lost hundreds of soldiers in the war. She had suffered through Indian raids on her frontiers. She had spent an enormous amount of money. And what her people wanted most now was peace and prosperity. They were bothered most by one part of the new British tax program—the sudden, strict enforcement of the Navigation Acts.

The Navigation Acts had been in existence for a hundred years. They provided that trade could be carried on only in English vessels (colonial ships were considered English) and only with English possessions. The colonials were thus forbidden to trade with the French, Dutch and Spanish islands in the West Indies. They must buy all their sugar and molasses, necessary for making rum, the common drink of the day, from such British islands as Jamaica, Antigua and Barbados. The acts provided that any products bought from such islands as French Guadeloupe and Martinique or Spanish Santo Domingo must be sent first to England and then shipped to the colonies, or a tax must be paid upon them equal to what it would have cost to send the cargo to England.

One trouble was that the British West Indian islands could not use all of the products of the colonies—the tar, turpentine, hemp, lumber, barrel staves and other products. A second thing was that sugar and molasses could often be purchased from 25 to 40 per cent cheaper in the foreign-held islands than in the British possessions. Both of these facts had made smuggling a highly profitable business. And so there had grown up over a long period of years a busy, illegal trade with the forbidden islands.

Even during the French and Indian War, though such trade was then actually treason, the smuggling had continued. The French West Indian islands desperately needed the provisions and products of the colonial mainland, and prices were high. Even "an investment of ten shillings would ordinarily bring a return of from fifty shillings to three pounds," a neat profit on a single voyage. With the stakes so high, the risks so little, many well-known merchants in Philadelphia founded great fortunes on the profits made from smuggling. And there was no coast better suited for this secret, illegal traffic than that of southern New Jersey.

The broken coastline, with its narrow, twisting rivers, its broad bays and many inlets guarded by shifting sandbars, was ideally made for a smuggler's paradise. From the Cohansey River and lower Delaware Bay, around Cape May and up the Atlantic coast, there were many isolated spots perfect for the landing of illegal cargoes. Coastal schooners, piloted by native seamen who knew every shifting sandbar as a modern man knows the streets of home, could pop in through the inlet passages, scoot across the wide bays and vanish up rivers winding through the dense pine and cedar forests of the mainland.

Little Egg Harbor became a hotbed of such activity. The winding Mullica River, branches of which wound two-thirds of the way across the state toward the Delaware, offered a perfect hiding place and a watery highway inland for smugglers wanting to get rid of their cargoes. At any one of a dozen landings along the Mullica, barrels of molasses and sugar, casks of tea or coffee or spices, were broken out of a smuggler's hold, placed on waiting wagons and carts and dragged along rough sand roads to Philadelphia.

The British sometimes tried to stop this traffic, but they always failed. The reason that they did was that there was hardly a revenue officer who could not be bought—and hardly a merchant who would not buy him. Customs posts usually were filled by "needy wretches who found it easier and more profitable not only to wink but to sleep in their beds; the Merchants' pay being more generous than the King's." Some idea of the large sums involved can be gained from official British figures on colonial imports for the years 1760 and 1761 during the heart of the French and Indian War. As the colonies were all growing, the imports

Smugglers would land their booty at wharves like this one

rose in all where smuggling was not a factor. But in Pennsylvania, for example, the figures actually showed *a drop* from 707,998 pounds sterling to 204,064 pounds. There can be little question that those 500,000 missing pounds sterling—and how much more no one could ever know—represented the smugglers' take.

When the war ended, King George III and his prime minister, Lord George Grenville, decided to put an end to all this. Grenville secured the passage of the Sugar Act of 1764, which cut in half the import duty on sugar from foreign islands. This was still much higher than the colonists thought fair. But Grenville was determined to see that the tax was collected. He called on the Royal Navy to police American ports and to seize ships and cargoes for disobeying the Navigation Acts. Other parts of the new laws almost outlawed manufacturing in the colonies. George III was going to milk what he called "his farms" in America, and it did not matter that the Americans might object to being milked. As one Englishman boasted: "The American today is apparelled from head to foot in our manufactures . . . he scarcely drinks, sits, moves, labours or recreates himself without contributing to the mother country."

This may have been fine for the mother country, but not for the colonials. New Jersey, like the other colonies, was soon stirring in opposition. The crackdown on smuggling especially threatened to cut off a lot of the colony's revenue. The old customs inspectors whom merchants had bought almost at will were fired by Grenville and replaced by honest dour Scotsmen known as "Scotch Laddys," who seemed content to live on their salaries. Enforcement of the Navigation Acts became so strict that one merchant moaned "the happy days of smuggling are over."

They were not over for long. The Royal Navy and the Scotch Laddys might be able to clamp tight controls on major ports like Boston, New York and Philadelphia, but those creeks and inlets along the Jersey shore were a different matter. Large naval vessels could not follow the flitting schooners and shallops through narrow channels and across treacherous shoals. The Scotch Laddys simply could not police every isolated woodland landing place. As the large amount of colonial goods in the British West Indies drove prices down, many merchants faced ruin. Farmers lost markets, lumber rotted on wharves, legal trade was almost at a standstill. There was only one way to survive, and it offered greater profits than ever—illegal trade with the French and Spanish islands in defiance of the Royal Navy, in defiance of the customs collectors.

The result was that smuggling picked up all along the inlet-dented New Jersey coast from Toms River to Cape May and around the cape along the lower shores of Delaware Bay. And with this new activity there went a new spirit of warlike resistance toward the King's men who tried to stop it.

One Jerseyman who acted as a spy on a Little Egg Harbor shallop in October, 1769, went to Philadelphia to give information to customs authorities, but his activities had become known. He was followed and seized by a group of sailors. First they tarred and feathered him from head to foot. Then they paraded him through the streets, passing first in front of the customs house, then in front of the home of the port collector. After this, they put their spy in a pillory, then finally rolled him in mud beside the dock before he was "let go in peace, to sin no more."

Even worse was what happened to a customs collector named John Hatton. Hatton was appointed in 1767 to the post of customs collector for the Cohansey district, which included Cape May. According to the accounts of the time, he was a difficult, hotheaded, quarrelsome man.

"Petty, overbearing and insolent," one of his neighbors called him—just the kind of man, especially in those times, to wind up in trouble.

Hatton was greatly impressed by his new title, and he began to make loud, fierce noises about all the horrible things he was going to do to the smugglers. He charged that three justices of the Common Pleas Court at Cape May —Thomas Leaming, John Leonard and James Wilden—were hand-in-glove with the smugglers. They were, he said, partners in a conspiracy with "certain Philadelphia merchants to smuggle goods through the Cape." He charged that "several thousand pounds worth of goods had recently been landed illegally" and that a wagonload of smuggled valuables had been carted past his own door in broad daylight under an escort of armed men who defied him to do anything about it. This was too much for Hatton; he went to Cape May to put a stop to the whole business.

In November, 1770, shortly after he arrived at the Cape, a ship named the *Prince of Wales* came into the bay and started to unload her cargo into several small pilot boats. Hatton, his son, and a Negro aide rowed out and saw the crew throw over "a great quantity of Bales and Casks of Clarett." When Hatton got close alongside, "they called out to me and bid me stand off or they would sink me, and they manned their sides with Swivels, Guns, Peteraries, Blunderbusses and Musketts, and declared they would murder us."

This show of force was too much even for Hatton. He decided to leave the *Prince of Wales* alone, but he set out after one of the smaller smuggling vessels bearing some of the unloaded cargo. This time he got aboard, found the craft full of illegal goods and seized her.

The smugglers, however, weren't the kind of men to let this happen right under their eyes. They sent out boats, boarded the vessel Hatton had seized and captured Hatton, his son and the Negro. "They took our guns," Hatton later wrote, "and with swords and axes beat us in a most inhuman manner, riffling our Pocketts, taking from me one riffle Pistol, four dollars and my Shoe buckles and other trifles."

The bruised and battered Hatton trio was put ashore, and the smugglers went about their business. But Hatton still wouldn't give up. He sent his son to Philadelphia to try to track down the smuggled goods. The son roamed the waterfront, spotted one of the smugglers, and went to the Philadelphia customs house for help. John Swift, the collector of customs, sent his own son back with young Hatton. Swift later described what happened to them.

Seven or eight sailors "arm'd with Clubbs" closed in upon young Hatton and Swift, who took to their heels, with the sailors in pursuit. "My son," Swift wrote, "was fortunate to get into a House where he was known & protected. Young Hatton likewise got into another House, but the Sailors follow'd & dragged him out, and drove him from place to place . . . and pour'd a pot of Tar upon his Head, and then feather'd him. The mob gathered as they drove him with sticks from Street to Street. They had a rope around his body, and when he would not walk or run, they drag'd him; they put him in the Pillory, and when they were tired of that, they drove him to the River and duck'd him. Then they put him into a Boat and row'd him across the River to the Jersey shore & there landed him."

The elder Hatton took his case to Governor William Franklin, the illegitimate son of Benjamin Franklin and the last royal governor of New Jersey. Franklin threw out the complaint. Hatton, he said, had a "very unhappy, violent temper, sometimes bordering on Madness, so that it is impossible he can live long with his neighbors."

Franklin's action only convinced Hatton more than ever that the whole world was against him. He felt that the courts were in league with the smugglers, and now even the Governor had turned him down on what, after all, was a clear-

William Franklin, the last royal governor of New Jersey, threw out Hatton's complaint

cut case. Hatton certainly had reason to feel as he did. The truth was that nobody wanted the smuggling stopped. It was a way of life, the only possible answer to a bad law, and much of the welfare of the colony depended upon it. The lowest classes and the best classes were engaged in it— and so even the governor ignored it.

New Jersey was growing and prospering, and the profits made from smuggling were only part of it. In 1766, at the forks of the Mullica, Charles Read founded the Batsto Iron Works. Read was collector of customs for the port of Burlington, and he knew well what was going on along the Mullica in the way of smuggling. In his official reports, he noted that "many Vessels trading to Plantations not belonging to the King of Great Britain, returning with cargoes of Rum, Sugar and Molasses, have found means to smuggle the same into His Majesty's Plantations, without paying the King's Duty." Read was accused of being in league with the smugglers, but the truth seems to be that he merely closed his eyes to their activities as almost everyone else did.

Read himself was excited by the idea of developing the first great iron foundries in the colony. There were deposits of "bog iron" under some of the south Jersey marshes, and Read founded furnaces at Batsto, Atsion, Etna and Taunton. The iron was of poor quality, and Read was eventually to go bankrupt. Before he did, his Batsto furnace became a major supplier of cannon balls for George Washington's armies.

Lying between New York and Philadelphia, New Jersey was influenced by the life and the trade of those two growing cities. The colony was a bridge, a pathway, between the two. Travel was by boat as much as possible, for the roads of the day, following old Indian trails for the most part, were narrow and twisting and bumpy. If one were traveling from New York to Philadelphia, it was customary to take a "stage boat" from New York to Perth Amboy. There the boat connected with an overland stage, or horse-drawn carriage, that took off over the bumpy country roads. The trip in the mid-1750s usually took from thirty to forty hours, providing the winds for the sail to Perth Amboy were fair. Later, this traveling time under favorable conditions was cut to twenty-four hours, which was thought remarkable speed for that time.

The stage routes were dotted with ordinaries. Here horses could be changed, and jolted travelers could rest. Since the ordinaries represented virtually the only contact with the outside world, they became the centers of much community life. Travelers from Philadelphia or New York, sipping their hot buttered rum, held forth on the latest developments in the growing struggle between the mother country and the colonies. Newspapers were few and the copies scarce, and so it was often in the ordinary that a traveler would hold up the latest copy and read to the gathering country crowd the news of the day. It was in the ordinaries

The Batsto Iron Works were founded at the fork of the Mullica River

that most New Jerseyans first heard the battle cry of the Revolution—"no taxation without representation"—and many a tavern owner became a leader in the cause.

If the ordinaries were a place where the feelings and patriotism of the common folk were expressed, there were other places of debate in New Jersey. One of the most important was Princeton University.

Education had gotten off to a slow start in New Jersey.

The Indian King Tavern, built in 1750, was one of the many ordinaries that dotted the King's Highway

This could hardly be avoided. The early settlers had to struggle to clear the land, plant their fields and build their homes. They had little time or opportunity for anything else. And so the first school of which there is any record was started in 1664, but it and others like it were nothing like the schools we know today.

Usually a school was started when a wandering teacher came into a town and offered to teach children in return for food and shelter. Such one-teacher schools, when they existed at all, limited themselves to teaching the basics of reading, writing and arithmetic. Since books were scarce, what became known as hornbooks were used. A sheet of paper on which were drawn the letters of the alphabet and some spelling words or arithmetic problems would be fastened on a board. Over this would be placed a very thin sheet of horn. The students could see the words and figures through the horn as through a piece of glass, but they would not be able to mark or tear the paper—and so a hornbook could. be used by student after student and would last for a long while.

As the colony prospered in the mid-1700s, the settlers began to seek better education for their children. And so, in 1746, Princeton University was started. At first, the president himself was the whole teaching staff, assisted by just one usher or janitor. Established first at Elizabethtown, the college later moved to Newark and finally, after ten years, to Princeton. In its first graduating class of six members in 1748 was Richard Stockton, later a New Jersey signer of the Declaration of Independence.

In the following years, many Revolutionary leaders went to Princeton. Among its graduates were Colonel Nathaniel Scudder, of Monmouth County, the only member of Congress to be killed during the Revolution; Alexander Macwhorter, the patriot leader of Newark; Dr. Benjamin Rush, of Philadelphia, the Revolutionary surgeon who was probably the most famous medical man of his day; Philip Freneau, the poet of the Revolution; Aaron Burr, a Revolutionary War officer and later Vice-President; James Madison, another Revolutionary officer who served on Washington's staff and later became the fourth President of the United States; and Colonel Henry (Light Horse Harry) Lee, one of the most dashing cavalry leaders of the Revolution.

In the same class with Burr, Madison and Lee was the Reverend Philip Vicars Fithian, of Greenwich, who was to be a leader in New Jersey's most colorful act of protest before the Revolution. Fithian was a scholar and he wrote of the men and life of his times. He left two journals that

An early view of Princeton showing Nassau Hall,

give vivid descriptions of colonial life. After he was graduated from Princeton, he lived for a time in Virginia, tutoring the children of the owner of a large plantation. He returned to New Jersey in late 1774. He was just in time.

The split between England and the colonies had now deepened and worsened. King George III and his ministers had refused to give up the idea that the American colonists must be taxed one way or another, whether they would or not. The Sugar Act had been followed by the Stamp Act— a law that called for the placing of a tax stamp on every legal document, every will and deed. The outcry over the Stamp Act led to its repeal, but the British government still

built in 1756, and the President's house

insisted on its right to tax. In 1767 the Townshend Acts were passed, taxing the main colonial imports—glass, red and white lead, paper, painters' colors and tea.

There was another storm of protest in the colonies, and finally, in 1773, Lord North proposed that the taxes be dropped on everything except tea. And he hoped to fix this tax so that the Americans wouldn't object. Money was returned to the British East India Company by the British government so that, even with the tax on the tea, the tea could still be sold cheaper in America than it could be smuggled from the West Indies. All that was left was the principle, the principle of the right to tax. Lord North did not expect trouble from the colonists over a mere principle.

He had some reason for thinking this. Tea at the time was the favorite household beverage in the colonies. It was thought that at least one million Americans drank tea twice a day. Almost every housewife, rich or poor, had to have her tea. Philadelphia women were said to be "such slaves to it that they would rather go without their dinners than without a dish of tea." Americans might object to the tea tax, but Lord North expected that the American woman's thirst for tea would conquer all.

He was wrong. The stubborn colonists refused to drink the tea as long as there was a tax upon it. In many a household, solemn vows were taken never to drink tea again.

Aaron Burr (left), an illustrious Princeton graduate, later became Vice-President of the United States. Philip Freneau, the Poet of the Revolution, was also a graduate of Princeton

From the plantations of Virginia to the rocky farms of Massachusetts, tea was banned from the dining room. Housewives who served it were shunned by their neighbors as unpatriotic. Other drinks were taken up, especially coffee, which has remained the favorite American household drink ever since.

Despite the outcry against the tea tax, the British sent over to America a number of ships loaded with the British East India Company tea. When the first of these ships reached Boston, a group of patriots disguised as Indians charged aboard, broke open the chests of tea and dumped the contents into the harbor. It was a deed that aroused all the colonies, that led to harsh British measures against Boston—and so to the Revolution.

Less famous but equally dramatic was New Jersey's own "tea party." In early December, 1774, only a month after Philip Vicars Fithian had returned to Greenwich, a British brig named the *Greyhound* made her way up the Cohansey River from Delaware Bay. The *Greyhound* was loaded with British tea, destined for Philadelphia. Her captain had learned, however, that other tea ships had been turned back, unable to unload their cargoes. Knowing that Greenwich had been a favorite smuggler's haven in the past, he decided to try to smuggle his tea ashore there.

It seemed like a good idea. There was a Tory, Daniel Bowen, himself a former skipper, who lived in a house by Market Square, only a short distance from the Greenwich wharf. Quietly, on the night of December 12, the tea-laden chests were taken from the *Greyhound*'s hold and hidden in the cellar of Bowen's home. It was all done in the small, dark hours of the night; it was all supposed to be extremely secret. But word soon got around.

On December 18, Fithian wrote in his journal: "Early last week a Quantity of Tea said to be shipped at Rotterdam was brought & privately stored at Dan Bowens in Green-

The "tea house" in Greenwich, where the tea was hidden late at night before it was burned

wich. . . ." A mass meeting of Cumberland County citizens was held at Bridgeton on December 22, 1774, to decide what to do about the tea. Fithian wrote that the citizens at the meeting named a committee of thirty-five "to examine into & take proper care of the aforesaid Goods."

The kind of "proper care" the citizens had in mind was made clear later that very night. A group of young Whigs, as the patriots were then called, gathered near Shiloh, about four miles from Greenwich, and rode to Fithian's home. When they left, they were all clad and painted like Indians.

Soon a file of twenty-three "Indians," waving torches, came upon Bowen's home, broke into his cellar and began to lug out the chests of tea. The chests were carried across the street to the village green, where they were broken open and set on fire. Soon the entire load of British East

India Company tea was going up in flames, and the " Indians" were whooping and hollering as they performed a war dance around the bonfire.

Today a granite monument in the Greenwich village square lists the names of the twenty-three patriotic tea burners, but at the time the deed caused a great outcry— and it wasn't quite safe to admit anything. The British East India Company brought suit, asking 1,200 pounds in damages for the destruction of the tea. But the patriots stayed together, raised money, hired skillful lawyers—and so delayed action on the suit until the Revolution put an end to all royal authority.

In a second effort to punish the tea burners, the case was taken before a grand jury, with the hope of getting convictions and jail sentences. Chief Justice Frederick Smyth gave what one of the tea burners called "a very Large Charge to the Grand Jury Concerning the times, & the burning of the tea. . . ." But the grand jury refused to take any action. Justice Smyth sent them out a second time, but again they refused. The reason was not hard to find: the jury was well packed with patriots. The foreman and several of the members were relatives of some of those "Indians" who had burned the tea—and they weren't about to take action against their own kin.

Only a few months away was the battle of Lexington and Concord and the start of the Revolution. Most of the Greenwich tea burners were soon to be in the Continental Army, and Philip Vicars Fithian himself was to lose his life, dying of fever after the disastrous Battle of Long Island in 1776. Soon New Jersey herself was to become a major battleground of the Revolution.

As early as October, 1775, New Jersey answered the call of the Continental Congress and raised two battalions of troops. Each battalion consisted of eight companies containing sixty-eight privates. These first troops were sent to garrison duty in New York and then upstate to the borders of Canada.

Though most of the early fighting was in New England, the spirit of rebellion in New Jersey grew steadily. At first, there were many who hoped that peace could be made with the Crown, but by the spring of 1776 the mood of the public had hardened into a general, growing demand for independence.

The Provincial Congress, meeting on June 22, 1776, reflected this mood by naming five delegates to represent New Jersey in the Continental Congress then gathering in Philadelphia. Those chosen were Richard Stockton, Abraham Clark, John Hart, Francis Hopkinson and John Witherspoon. They were given these positive instructions: "We empower you to join with them [the delegates of the other colonies] in declaring the United Colonies independent of Great Britain. . . ." The Declaration of Independence was adopted on July 4, 1776. On August 2, the five New Jersey delegates were among those who added their names to the document under the great sprawling signature of John Hancock, the president of the Continental Congress.

For New Jersey the darkest and most desperate hours lay immediately ahead. Before the year was out, the entire state from the Hudson to the Delaware was to know the trampling feet of conquering British armies, but those independent, stiff-necked New Jerseyans—those rebels who had earlier touched off two minor "revolutions" of their own— were not the kind of men to quit. A flame lived in them that was to last and endure through eight long, hard years of war until independence at last was won.

Five New Jersey delegates signed the Declaration of Independence at the bottom of the fifth column: Richard Stockton, Joseph Witherspoon, Francis Hopkinson, John Hart, and Abraham Clark

BIBLIOGRAPHY

ANDREWS, CHARLES M., *The Colonial Period of American History*, Vol. III, *The Settlements*. New Haven: Yale University Press, 1937.

FISHER, GEORGE PARK, *The Colonial Era*. New York: Charles Scribner's Sons, 1903.

GIPSON, LAWRENCE HENRY, *The Coming of the Revolution*. New York: Harper and Row, 1954.

JOHNSON, ROBERT G., "Memoir of John Fenwick," *Proceedings New Jersey Historical Society*. First series, Vol. IV, No. II, pp. 53–89.

KEMMERER, DONALD L., *Path to Freedom*. Princeton: Princeton University Press, 1940.

KNOLLENBERG, BERNHARD, *Origin of the American Revolution*. New York: The Macmillan Company, 1960.

LEE, FRANCIS BAZLEY, *New Jersey as a Colony and as a State*. Vols. I, II. New York: The Publishing Society of New Jersey, 1902.

PARKER, R. WAYNE, "New Jersey in the Colonial Wars," *Proceedings of the New Jersey Historical Society*. N. S., Vol. VI, No. 4.

PIERCE, ARTHUR D., *Smugglers' Woods*. New Brunswick: Rutgers University Press, 1960.

POMFRET, JOHN E., *The Province of East Jersey, 1609–1702*. Princeton: Princeton University Press, 1962.

SMITH, SAMUEL, *The History of the Colony of Nova Caesaria, or New Jersey* (to the year 1721). Spartanburg, S.C.: The Reprint Company.

STOCKTON, FRANK R., *Stories of New Jersey*. New Brunswick: Rutgers University Press, 1961.

WERTENBAKER, THOMAS JEFFERSON, *The Middle Colonies*. New York: Charles Scribner's Sons, 1938.

IMPORTANT DATES

1609—Henry Hudson explores New Jersey coast.

1621—Captain Cornelis Jacobsen Mey names Cape May and builds fort at Red Bank on the Delaware.

1630—Dutch establish trading posts in north Jersey.

1634—First British explore Delaware Bay and River.

1638—Swedes enter the Delaware and soon afterward establish trading posts in New Jersey.

1642—Earl Plowden comes to New Jersey, but fails to establish a colony.

1643—Slaughter of Tappan Indians by Dutch in north Jersey touches off Indian war.

1651—Peter Stuyvesant attacks Swedes in the Delaware; four years later conquers them.

1664—English seize New York and New Jersey from Dutch; Duke of York gives all of New Jersey to Berkeley and Carteret; Middletown and Shrewsbury are settled.

1665—Philip Carteret arrives as first governor; Elizabethtown is settled.

1666—Puritans settle Newark; Woodbridge and Piscataway also founded.

1668—First assembly meets, passes stern penal code.

1672—Settlers in first rebellion name Captain James Carteret governor and "President of the Country."

1673—Dutch retake New York and New Jersey, but a year later British regain the colonies.

1674—Major Edmund Andros becomes governor of New York and New Jersey.

1675—John Fenwick settles Salem for the Quakers.

1676—Andros arrests Fenwick and holds him in prison in New York.

1677—Quakers settle Burlington, the capital of West Jersey.

1679—Andros arrests Governor Philip Carteret and a year later is recalled for his high-handed acts.

1693—Famous Fullerton-Jones law suit is started over disputed land titles.

1700—The so-called first revolution takes place in Middletown and is followed a year later by riot at trial of pirate Moses Butterworth.

1702—Queen Anne takes over government of colony from the proprietors and appoints her cousin, Lord Cornbury, as the first royal governor. War breaks out with France, and French privateers raid the New Jersey coast.

1708—Lord Cornbury is recalled in disgrace.

1738—New Jersey gets own royal governor for first time; Lewis Morris is named to post.

1741—New Jersey troops die of fever in campaign against Cartagena in West Indies.

1745—"Second revolution" breaks out in riots over land titles and quit rents.

1746—Princeton University is founded, trains many Revolutionary leaders.

1750—Quakers are the first to oppose slavery in New Jersey.

1754–1763—Hundreds of New Jersey troops die in the French and Indian War; Indians raid and scalp on the northern New Jersey frontier.

1766—Charles Read establishes the Batsto Iron Works in South Jersey, where cannon balls are soon to be made for General Washington's Revolutionary Army.

1774—Greenwich holds its own "tea party" as patriots, disguised as Indians, burn British East India Company's tea, and New Jersey prepares to go to war.

1775—Battle of Lexington and Concord.

1776—Declaration of Independence proclaimed on July 4.

PLACES TO VISIT

Readers may wish to visit the following historical sites in New Jersey.

ALLAIRE STATE PARK   Allaire has been developed as a park and recreation area and may be reached from an exit of the Garden State Parkway west of Belmar. The village, long deserted before it was acquired for park purposes, flourished in the first half of the nineteenth century, but many of the shops and buildings in the present park re-create the atmosphere of the early colonial period. Daily, except January 1, Thanksgiving and Christmas Day, 9 A.M. until dark. There is a standard fee when buildings are open.

BATSTO   Reached from another exit of the Garden State Parkway, Batsto is an authentic deserted village. Though the area was most prosperous in the early decades of the 1800's, the original iron forges date from colonial times and made cannon balls for Washington's Army during the Revolution. Many of the old buildings, dating from the colonial and Revolutionary War era, stand much as they did when they were ultimately abandoned and convey an authentic feeling of the past. Daily May 30–Labor Day, 10 A.M.– 6 P.M. Daily from day after Labor Day–April 30, 11 A.M.–6 P.M., except January 1, Thanksgiving and Christmas Day. Adults, $1; ages 12–18, 25¢; under 12, 10¢. Grounds free.

FREEHOLD   At West Main and Ninth Streets, the Moreau House served as the heaquarters for the British General Sir Henry Clinton during the Battle of Monmouth. The house was built about 1755 and is furnished in pre-Revolutionary War style. It is being restored.

GREENWICH   The town of Greenwich, with its tea party monument, still retains much of the flavor of its historic past.

HADDONFIELD   Built around 1747, the John Gill House at 343 Kings Highway East, is now maintained by the Haddonfield Historical Society. Tuesday and Thursday, 2–5 P.M. Other days by appointment. Closed July–August and holidays. Phone 429-7375. Free.

HOLMDEL   The Hendrickson House on Longstreet Road was built in the latter seventeeth and early eighteenth centuries. It is furnished in pre-1750 colonial style, even to storage and work space in the basement. Tuesday and Thursday, 1–5 P.M., June–September. Free.

MIDDLETOWN   On Kings Highway is located Marlpit Hall, built originally in 1684 with an addition in 1712. It is furnished in the style of the period up to 1750. Tuesday, Thursday and Saturday, 11 A.M.–5 P.M. Sunday 2–5 P.M. Open all year except June. Closed January 1, Thanksgiving and Christmas Day.

MORRISTOWN   Jockey Hollow National Park is on the site of the camp in which Washington's Army spent one of the worst winters of the Revolutionary War. Most of the emphasis is on the war period, but there is included in the park an old colonial mansion furnished in authentic pre-Revolutionary War style. Also in Morristown are two famous colonial homes, the Ford Mansion and the Schuyler-Hamilton House, both furnished in colonial style.

NORTH HACKENSACK   The Demarest House on Main Street, built in 1678, is furnished in colonial style.

SANDY HOOK STATE PARK   Now a seashore recreation area, the park is open to the public. The old lighthouse is no longer used, but it is open to visitors. It stands much as did the original light established there in pre-Revolutionary days. Nearby are the Twin Lights on the heights above Highlands, the area where Henry Hudson's men first landed and refilled their water casks. Though the Twin Lights were constructed in a later period, one gets a vivid impression from this height of why the area was known, in colonial days, as Neversinks. That is how far the heights were visible to sailors at sea.

SHREWSBURY   The Allen House, dating from the latter 1600's, was only recently acquired by the Monmouth County Historical Society and is in the process of restoration as a typical colonial home.

TRENTON   The William Trent House on Warren Street was built in 1709 and furnished in the style of the colonial period up to 1750. A faithful and authentic example of a home of the colonial times. Monday–Saturday: May–August, 10 A.M.–5 P.M.; September–April, to 4 P.M.; Sunday, all year from 1 P.M.; closed January 1, Thanksgiving, Christmas Day. Adults, 25¢; ages 7–11, 10¢.

WAYNE TOWNSHIP (outside Paterson)   The Dey Mansion, built between 1740–50, was one of Washington's headquarters during the Revolution. It is furnished in colonial fashion. Tuesday, Wednesday, Friday, 1–5 P.M.; Saturday and Sunday from 10 A.M.; also Monday and Thursday if holiday, 10 A.M.–5 P.M. Closed January 1, Thanksgiving, Christmas Day. Adults, 25¢; ages 12–17, 10¢; under 12, free.

Times and admission prices are subject to change.

INDEX